William Allen White, left, on the streets of Emporia.

FROM EMPORIA

THE STORY OF

William Allen White

Beverley Olson Buller

 KANSAS CITY STAR BOOKS

DEDICATION

For Daddy. You were right.

Beverley Olson Buller grew up reading and writing in Winfield, Kansas,
but has spent her adult life in getting kids to read and write as a teacher
and librarian in Newton, Kansas. Her professional motto is,
"Anyone can love reading if they find the right book."

Published by Kansas City Star Books
1729 Grand Boulevard
Kansas City, MO 64108

All rights reserved
Copyright © 2007 Beverley Olson Buller

No part of this book may be reproduced, stored in a retrieval system or transmitted
in any form or by any means, electronic, mechanical, photocopying, recording or
otherwise, without the prior consent of the publisher.

First Edition

ISBN 978-1-933466-46-0
Library of Congress Control Number: 2007932513
Editor: Monroe Dodd
Designer: Jean Dodd

Printed in the United States of America
by Walsworth Publishing Co., Inc.
Marceline, Mo.

CONTENTS

Learn More About It
Source Notes
llustration Sources
Index
Acknowledgments
Timeline (inside cover)

Man of Emporia, man of the world: William Allen White with Albert Einstein. Each received an honorary degree from Harvard in 1935.

INTRODUCTION

These days, William Allen White's name is not often heard outside his home state of Kansas. In his lifetime it was heard around the world.

Introducing himself as the new editor and owner of the Emporia *Gazette* newspaper in 1895, he made a promise:

"He hopes to always sign 'from Emporia' after his name, when he is abroad, and he trusts that he may so endear himself to the people that they will be as proud of the first words of the signature as he is of the last words."

When William Allen White wrote these words he was 27 and had never traveled west of the Rocky Mountains or east of the Mississippi. His writing had received only local acclaim. Obviously he intended to live a life that would reach throughout the world, even as it remained based in Kansas. He succeeded.

ENTIRELY PERSONAL.
To the gentle reader, who may, through the coming years during which we are spared to one another, follow the course of this paper, a word of personal address from the new editor of the GA-ZETTE, is due. In the first place, the new editor hopes to live here until he is the old editor, until some of the visions which rise before him as dreams, shall have come true. He hopes always to sign "from Emporia" after his name, when he is abroad, and he trusts that he may so endear himself to the people, that they will be as proud of the first words of the signature as he is of the last words. He

In the nearly half-century that he was editor of the *Gazette* he brought the world to Emporia through his widely reprinted editorials, his travel, his service to his country and his famous visitors. And he took Emporia to the world. His hometown was with him wherever he traveled, in whatever he said, and certainly in his writing. As a New York *Times* correspondent observed after his death, "To him the great world was only an extension of Emporia, and therefore he was a great citizen of the world."

If he were alive today, William Allen White would be a frequent flier. From Emporia he traveled innumerable times by train to New York, Chicago and Washington, D.C., conducting business. Before his death he had seen Europe on several occasions, as well as Asia and Haiti.

Politics, whether local or national, consumed him. He met 10 presidents, counting many as friends, and all Kansas governors from the time of statehood. Although he never graduated from college, eight universities, including Harvard, awarded him honorary degrees. Twenty of his books were published in his lifetime, two were made into movies and his writing earned two Pulitzer prizes. At the time of his 70th birthday, *Life* magazine called him "an American institution". When he died, the current president telegrammed his feelings of personal loss to the family, and newspapers around the world proclaimed the news in their headlines.

How did a man who lived in a small Kansas town in the years before television and the internet become so famous? Turn the page. Read all about it!

Kansas in the late 1860s,
when some counties in the far
west had not been organized.
William Allen White was born
in Emporia in Lyon County.
When he was still an infant,
his family moved to El Dorado
in Butler County. Dressed in
a fancy style of the day, his
portrait was made in the middle
1870s.

An Editor is Born

*I*n 1868, this birth announcement appeared in the Emporia *News*:

"There is another man in town they call Pap. He wears a stove pipe hat and carries a cane, and weighs (since the event) eight hundred pounds."

The man swollen with pride was Dr. Allen White. The reason was the birth on February 10, 1868, of a son, William Allen White. Birth certificates did not exist in those days, but it is appropriate that the future editor's arrival was recognized by the local newspaper.

"Willie," as he was called in his early years, was the first child of Mary Ann Hatten White and Dr. White. He was born within a year of their marriage.

Willie's father, a native of Ohio, had lost both his parents as a teenager. He worked as a store clerk, a school teacher and a tailor before graduating from medical school in Cleveland, Ohio. Allen White came to Emporia in 1859, when Kansas was still a territory.

Allen White and Mary Hatten White, William Allen White's parents, about the time of their marriage.

Willie's mother, also without parents by her teen years, was born in Canada, and spent 10 years at Knox College in Galesburg, Illinois, working off and on to support herself while living with another family. While in Galesburg, she heard Abraham Lincoln speak. When the new Kansas State Normal School for Teachers opened in 1865, she traveled to Emporia by stagecoach. That same year she met Allen White at a dance.

The Whites' marriage certificate from their wedding in Michigan.

They must have seemed like an odd couple. She was 35, petite and trim. He was 46, not much taller than she, but he weighed 220 pounds. She was quick-tempered; he was easy-going and slow to anger. Despite their differences, both loved books, both had hated slavery and both possessed strong wills.

Mary Ann, unable to find a room in Emporia so she could attend the college, instead took a job teaching school in nearby Council Grove, Kansas. Before she arrived, the school admitted only white children. Mary Ann, however, announced that she would welcome children of any color. That made some residents unhappy, which led to a battle that ended in court. In the end, her policy was upheld.

Within two years, Mary Ann returned to Illinois, and Allen wrote to her there. After a short correspondence, the two were engaged. In a letter written less than a month before the wedding, Allen assured Mary Ann: "You say you can't see or would like to know what it was that I saw in you that was attractive. Your History, together with that auburn hair and pink complexion are sufficient attraction for me."

They married on April 15, 1867, in Michigan, where Mary Ann's sister lived. Then they settled in Emporia, where Allen owned a house and part of a general store.

When Willie was barely a year old, his father decided Emporia was getting too crowded and moved the family to El

"The streets are full of emigrant wagons all the time ... The country about here is nearly all settled. It is astonishing how fast they can build towns out here."

Dorado, a town with less than a hundred people.

El Dorado was about 60 miles southwest of Emporia, and the trip was perilous for the baby. As the family crossed a stream, Willie was thrown from the wagon. Wrapped in a large shawl, he floated for a few seconds before he was rescued.

Mary Ann described her new home in a letter to a friend in 1879:

"The streets are full of emigrant wagons all the time, most of them going south. The country about here is nearly all settled. It is astonishing how fast they can build towns out here. We are within sixty-five miles of a railroad now and expect to have one here in less than two years, so you can see we are no longer on the frontier."

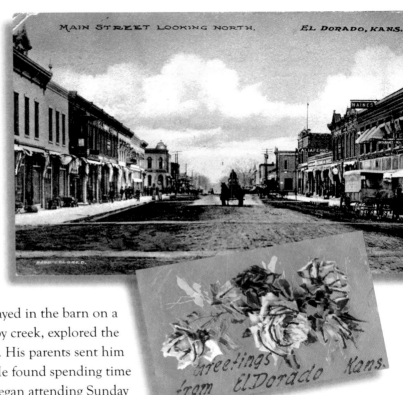

Allen White opened a store and became active in organizing the government of the little town, which became the county seat thanks to his help. A second child, Freddie, was born to the Whites in El Dorado but did not live to see his first birthday.

Willie grew up an only child, usually commanding the full attention of his mother. He played in the barn on a makeshift trapeze, swam in a nearby creek, explored the woods and romped on the prairies. His parents sent him to Sunday school at an early age. He found spending time with other boys such fun that he began attending Sunday schools in three other churches. He was a shy child, chubby, with a crop of red hair and a face that frequently wore a smile.

William Allen White later gave his mother full credit for starting him as a writer. To make their El Dorado home warmer in the winter, she pasted newspapers on the walls. Little Willie could pick out letters from the advertisements. She read to him and, as he grew, with him. As the city grew, she

*Willie as a
little boy.*

helped found the El Dorado City Library.

By the time Willie was 6 and ready to start classes in
the town's large stone schoolhouse, he was reluctant to leave
his mother. However, his mind was soon changed by games
of marbles and hide-and-seek with the other boys, by the joy
of recess on the prairie within a hundred yards of the school
— and by a crush on his first teacher. Teachers discovered
he moved rapidly through the readers and already knew his
multiplication tables.

Allen White, meanwhile, was busy supporting his family
and promoting his growing town. Since coming to El Dorado,
he had twice been elected to the city council and served
as its treasurer. His general store evolved into a successful
drugstore. He sold it when Willie was 6 and used the money to move his family to a
farm outside town. There, Allen recreated the log cabin of his childhood, complete
with dirt floor. Now 50 years old, he hired laborers to do most of the work.

On the farm, Willie milked cows, fed pigs, and
chopped wood.

Within two years, however, the difficulty of
keeping hired help and the added work for Mary Ann
White brought the Whites back to town.

Allen's investments in El Dorado real estate
paid off handsomely. A house with six bedrooms
and big porches on a large lot was built for the
family, and, because of his fondness for playing

OFFICE OF

The White House,

DR. ALLEN WHITE, PROP'R.

This House is Newly Built and Furnished
Thro'out. Special Pains taken for Comfort of
Guests. Good Sample Rooms in the House.

El Dorado, Kan., _____ 188___

*The Whites' house in El Dorado was big enough to rent out rooms, bringing the family extra
income.*

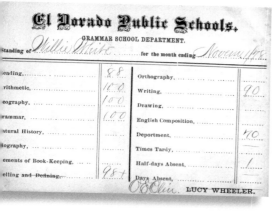

El Dorado Public Schools.
GRAMMAR SCHOOL DEPARTMENT.
Standing of *Willie White* for the month ending *November 1885*

Reading	88	Orthography		
Arithmetic	100	Writing	90	
Geography	100	Drawing		
Grammar	100	English Composition		
Natural History		Deportment	70	
Biography		Times Tardy		
Elements of Book-Keeping		Half-days Absent	1	
Spelling and Defining	98+	Days Absent		

LUCY WHEELER.

the host, Allen White opened a hotel in it. After a few years, Mary Ann tired of cooking and cleaning for all the visitors, and the Whites stopped taking in paying guests.

The White family lived on in the large house with the big yard, and Willie began to be called Will as he grew. At 7, Will broke his shoulder blade in a fall from a horse, ending his interest in anything athletic. He found other things to occupy his time.

He captured a raccoon and a bird and kept them as pets in a shed on the property, and for his 12th birthday his parents gave him a small organ on which he taught himself to play popular songs by ear. Mary Ann insisted on music lessons until it became obvious Will was not reading the notes on the sheet music. Nevertheless, music always remained a part of his life. As an adult, he would play a large piano in his home — still by ear. Will discovered the books of Mark Twain and still attended three Sunday schools.

Receipt for the organ Will's parents bought for his 12th birthday.

Will remembered himself as "...a pudgy, middle-sized boy who clowned a bit to disguise his awkwardness...fairly good in his studies...lower in deportment than anything else, indicating something which his parents called mischievousness and the teacher probably catalogued as meanness...."

When Allen attended political meetings, Will sometimes went along. Once the railroad was built to El Dorado, visitors to the White home included Elizabeth Cady Stanton and Susan B. Anthony, in Kansas campaigning for women's rights, and Kansas congressmen from Washington, D.C., who were known to Allen.

Will got his first paying job at age 12 at the insistence of his father, who sent him to work for the summer at a small weekly newspaper in which Allen White had invested money. For $1.50 a week, Will rolled ink across the type on a small press, carried water from the well, folded papers for subscribers and swept the floors each evening.

Even at a young age, Will carried a business card.

After less than two weeks on the job, Will discovered his father was paying his wages. Disgusted at the fact it wasn't a "real" paycheck, he promptly left the newspaper office and rejoined his friends at the swimming hole. He also raised vegetables and sold them from a cart downtown. That put some money in his little mechanical iron bank, which was shaped like a fat man in a suit, his hand extended to accept coins. Records of the El Dorado Public Library from December 1880 to June 1881 show he was an ambitious young reader, checking out such books as *Arabian Nights, Tom Sawyer, Gulliver's Travels, Don Quixote, The Last of the Mohicans, Little Women* and *Robinson Crusoe.*

In his early teenage years Will began to write poetry, inspired by poems he read in schoolbooks, newspapers, and magazines. He also began to court his first girlfriend, Agnes Riley, who had a poem published in the local newspaper. He went door to door, selling subscriptions to a children's magazine, and he began to talk seriously with his father about politics and about growing up.

Will's iron bank.

An autograph from Will's first love.

Yet on October 4, 1882, Allen White died, possibly as a result of diabetes. Only a few months before, Allen had been elected mayor of El Dorado, and townspeople thronged to his funeral.

Reading his father's books helped Will fill the empty space.

"I have never ceased to sorrow that he did not stay with me for another twenty years," Will wrote as an adult, "to help me and to guide me from the follies which he may have seen ahead of me."

It was not to be. At 14 years of age, Will was rushed into adulthood.

Chapter Two

Man of the House

With his father gone, Will took on new and important duties. He learned to deposit money, manage a bank account and collect rent from the properties his father had owned.

"At fourteen, I was the man of the house," Will wrote in his autobiography. "I took to responsibility as a duck takes to water."

It didn't take long for his mother to realize that the family needed more income. Because their spacious home had extra bedrooms, she began to take

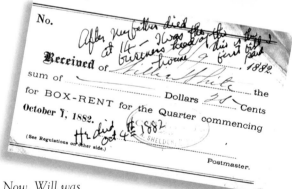

Now, Will was paying the family bills.

in boarders. One of those boarders began to mold Will's future. He was former State Senator T.B. "Bent" Murdock, who ran the El Dorado *Republican* newspaper. He brought with him a baby daughter and a young wife

15

Will's mentor, "Bent" Murdock.

whose love of books fanned the flame established in Will by his mother.

"I used to go to their room and sit with her beside the glow of the glittering base-burner while she read to me beautifully," Will remembered. The relationship continued even after the Murdocks bought a substantial home on a hill above town and grew in social prominence in El Dorado. Murdock's involvement in local and state politics, the couple's position in the community and their travels left a lasting impression on Will.

"I was proud of him," he recalled, "grafted him into the wound that death had left when my father went, and gave him a son's affection and respect which I never withheld."

As he entered high school, Will discovered he enjoyed singing and joined a group of other boys in a quartet. He also continued playing the piano, sometimes earning $2 a night at square dances. If he called the square dances he would earn an extra dollar. The city library became a place to meet friends and find classic books such as *A Tale of Two Cities* and *Les Miserables*.

At 16, he graduated from El Dorado High School. After Will spent one last summer swimming in the creek and reading on the big front porch of the house, college beckoned. The president of the College of Emporia, looking for students, visited the White home one day and Will's mother decided he should attend. A room was found for him in the home of an Emporia widow with several children, and

Emporia public library.

he began taking classes in Latin and Greek, advanced algebra, physics and English literature. The public library provided books and magazines, and the Congregational Church occupied his Sundays — although, as in boyhood, he went to a different church for Sunday school.

Despite enjoying the experience, Will recalled that by the end of the school year he concluded that "a big, healthy, strapping seventeen year old boy had no business to let his mother keep boarders to send him to school."

Intending to find a job back in El Dorado, he wrote three identical application letters to owners of a general store, a grocery and a newspaper. Only the newspaper editor replied that he had an opening, so Will hired on at the Butler County *Democrat*. Without realizing it, at age 17 he had set off on his life's career.

Will worked for $3 a week as a printer's devil, or helper, doing many of the same jobs that he had done in his few weeks of newspaper employment as

University Hall on Mount Oread, heart of the KU campus in the 1880s, when Will was enrolled there.

a child. After a month of steady work his pay rose to
$4 a week, and he began to learn to set type and write
local items. By Christmas, with newspaper skills and his
mother's encouragement, he quit the job, enrolled for
spring semester 1886 at the College of Emporia, and took
a printing job at the Emporia *News*. That summer found him back in El Dorado
working as a reporter for Bent Murdock's newspaper, the El Dorado *Republican*.

Fall 1886 brought more change to Will and his mother. Will's best friend
from the College of Emporia had moved to the University of Kansas in
Lawrence, and Will decided to follow. His mother rented out the big family
home in El Dorado and moved to a smaller
house in Lawrence close to the university so
Will could have a place to live, along with home
cooking. While in Lawrence, Will found work
reporting university news for the Lawrence
Journal and eventually the university's literary
paper. The summer after his first year at KU, he
returned to work for Murdock in El Dorado.
It was that summer that he discovered *Roget's
Thesaurus*, a reference book he used the rest of
his professional life.

Will's University of Kansas academic record, from a copy sent to him years later at his request.

Will dove into university life in his
second year, joining a fraternity, attending
music programs and reporting on campus events for several area newspapers.
His grades were average, ranging from A's in English and history to F's in
mathematics. That summer, he stayed in Lawrence to work for the *Tribune*.

1888 marked the beginning of Will's last full year in college, although he
did not know it when he started school that
fall. He continued to enjoy newspaper work
and extracurricular activities but dropped math
classes, which he was never able to pass. At
KU, he met fellow students who would later
become state and national leaders. By working

Clowning around for a photographer in the Rockies in 1889, these young men got serious later in life. For this pose, Will stood fourth from the left, hatless and looking down. Among his posturing pals around the table were a future governor of Missouri, an attorney general of Oklahoma, professors at Stanford, MIT and Michigan, a banker and a future major general in the U.S. Army.

extra hard, he earned the money to travel to Colorado in summer 1889 with some of those friends.

They spent the summer camping in what is now Rocky Mountain National Park, hunting for food and climbing mountains, including 14,500-foot Longs Peak.

"If I ever grew up and became a man," Will wrote later, "it was the summer of 1889, in Colorado, in a little log cabin filled with a dozen boys on the

Kansas City in the early 1890s, where Will ventured for a taste of life in the city.

Big Thompson River."

Little wonder that college held no appeal for Will that fall. In December 1889, his mentor, Bent Murdock, asked him to take over the El Dorado *Republican* for $18 a week while Murdock served as a state senator in Topeka.

Will's mother and his favorite professors argued for him to finish college, but the pull of the newspaper was too strong. He and his mother moved into one of the smaller homes they owned in El Dorado, and Will moved into the role of small-town editor on a newspaper owned by someone else.

With the freedom the position gave him, Will blossomed. He was a little taller than five feet seven inches and by his own admission a little fat, but he spent what money he could on the latest styles in men's clothing.

During the day, he wrote editorials and local items, found advertisers for the paper and oversaw the work of the staff. In the evenings, he joined boating parties on the Walnut River, played music with others, and visited the local ice cream parlor.

He began to write poetry and publish it in the *Republican*, where it was picked up and reprinted in the Kansas City *Star* and then in newspapers in other parts of the country. The name William Allen White traveled outside of Kansas long before the man.

In summer 1891, after attending the state Republican convention for the first time, Will

Sallie Lindsay

Blitz, illegal voting; R. E. Bruner, using the mails to defraud; James R. Benegar, attempting to defraud the pension bureau.

White-Lindsay.

Will A. White of THE STAR and Miss Sallie Lindsay were married this morning at 10 o'clock at the home of the bride, 338 Waverly avenue, Kansas City, Kas. The ceremony was performed, in the presence of relatives only, by the Rev. Charles R. Mitchell of the Grand Avenue Methodist Episcopal church. Mr. and Mrs. White started at 1 o'clock for Las Vegas, N. M., and expect to be absent for some weeks.

Switchman Coffey's Injuries Fatal.

John Coffey, a Memphis switchman who

wrote the first of many editorials that would bring him to the attention of the nation. It was called "The Regeneration of Colonel Hucks," and was the sentimental story of an old Civil War veteran returning to the Republican Party. Within a week, it had been reprinted in newspapers throughout Kansas and gone on to newspapers across the country.

Before that summer was over, job offers came in from two Kansas City newspapers, and he chose the Kansas City *Journal* at a salary of $25 a week. Twenty-three-year-old Will boarded the train alone and headed for the big city.

Living in a rented room with two friends who also had come to town, Will enjoyed the music, food, and drama of Kansas City. One night, at a friend's insistence, he visited the home of a beautiful young teacher named Sallie Lindsay. Born in Kentucky, Sallie was one of 10 children of a Confederate officer.

Her cooking and love of books drew Will to her home again and again, until he moved to Topeka in spring 1892 to work as a statehouse correspondent for the *Journal*. Regular letters went back and forth as Will covered Kansas politics, traveling around the state. After less than a year, Will quit his job at the *Journal* over the placement of an article he thought should have been front-page news. The next day he got a job at the Kansas City *Star*. The *Star* was a respected paper, and it brought him back to Kansas City. His mother arrived, too, and they bought a large house. Now Sallie could visit their home, and she and Will could attend theater and musical programs.

On April 27, 1893, Will and Sallie

Will and Sallie in the 1890s, early in their life together.

Will's Kansas City bank.

were married in the parlor of her parents' Kansas City home and started their life together with a trip by train to New Mexico and Colorado. Eventually, Will's mother and some members of Sallie's family joined the couple in Colorado.

They stayed so long that the *Star* gave Will's job to someone else. Meanwhile, the bank where they kept their money failed. Several days later, the *Star* telegraphed Will that they needed him back. The White family returned to Kansas City and the newspaper life.

Will's first year of married life was eventful. He and a friend, Albert Bigelow Paine, published a small book of poetry called *Rhymes by Two Friends*. When the *Star* began to publish a Sunday paper, he wrote stories and poetry as well as feature articles for it. Will met the first of many presidents he would encounter when he was assigned to report on William McKinley as his train came through Kansas City.

In that first year Sallie assumed an important role that lasted through their married life: the constant partner in the career of William Allen White. Will was the first to acknowledge it.

"Sallie was always reading to me the books of the hour and the magazines of the day," he recalled. "There were hours of tall talk before I wrote, and afterwards while we were revising what I wrote."

Despite the excitement of the city and the success of Will's writing, things didn't feel permanent. As he put it: "My heart was in Kansas and I wanted to be my own master."

By 1895, he and Sallie began to look for a Kansas newspaper they could afford to buy and that was in a college town. They found both in the Emporia *Gazette*.

With help from Will's mother and friends from Will's years covering Kansas politics, they purchased the paper for $3,000 and began making plans to go to Emporia. The move would last them the rest of their lives.

Chapter Three

The New Editor

W illiam Allen White was 27 years old and had $1.25 in his pocket when he stepped off the train in Emporia. The day was June 1, 1895.

As the new editor of the Emporia *Gazette* Will wanted to make an impression on future subscribers. So he spent 25 cents to hire a horse and wagon to take him and his baggage to a boarding house. That way, no one would see him walking.

The next morning, he visited the *Gazette* and found a small but well-kept building with one press. That afternoon he wrote an editorial introducing "the new editor" to his readers. He expressed hope that he would live in Emporia until he was the old editor. Also, he said the *Gazette's* columns would reflect the average person reading it. Political opinions, he said, would be restricted to the

Assuming a noble pose beside a wicker basket full of discarded manuscripts, Will sat for a photographer.

Home of the Gazette *when Will bought it in 1895.*

editorial page.

As people were reading this, Will was making himself known on the streets of Emporia, picking up advertising and gathering local news for the next issue. At the end of that first week, his wife and mother joined him. They moved into a six-room house rented for $18 a month.

Sallie went to the *Gazette* each day. She wrote stories for the paper about people in Emporia — who was getting married, who was celebrating an anniversary, or who was welcoming a new baby. She also continued as partner to her husband, reading and editing everything he wrote.

Money was tight that first summer, but they found a way to supplement the *Gazette*'s earnings. Will's articles sometimes were reprinted in other newspapers around the United States, and before long offers came from publishers in New York and Chicago to collect the articles in a book.

Will and Sallie's first home in Emporia.

24

has gained in wealth and in population while Kansas has gone down hill. Colorado has gained in every way while Kansas has lost in every way since 1888. What is the matter with Kansas?

Excerpt from the editorial that propelled William Allen White to national fame.

The Whites chose a Chicago publisher, gathered more stories and received a $500 advance on the book called *The Real Issue*. Some of that money they promptly used to help pay back the bank loan for the *Gazette*. About then, Will was hired by the Kansas City *World* to cover his first national Republican convention. For the rest of their lives, the Whites always enjoyed income beyond what they made from the *Gazette*.

Meanwhile, Will worked 12-hour days to make the *Gazette* reflect the promises he made in that first editorial. He trimmed extra words out of articles and focused on Emporia news. On Mondays the *Gazette* began to carry a column of church news, and once a week the children in town had their own column. Will paid to have major news sent immediately by telegraph from around the United States, rather than copying and printing it days later from other newspapers. By the first anniversary of the Whites' ownership, the *Gazette* had added 300 new subscribers, repaid $214 on its bank loan and added a "job shop" to handle various printing jobs for local businesses.

Early in his second year as editor of the *Gazette*, Will wrote the editorial that would make him famous nationwide. In an opinion piece finished hurriedly so he could catch a train to meet his wife in Colorado, Will sarcastically voiced disgust at the political scene in Kansas. He handed it over to be set in type and headed out of town.

By the time the editorial, entitled "What's the Matter with Kansas?" showed up in the *Gazette* on August 15, 1896, he was in Colorado. On his return, he found a fat stack of letters from all over the country, most of them filled with praise.

"What's the Matter with Kansas?" was reprinted in newspapers nationwide and was used in campaigns by the Republican Party on both national and state levels. As White wrote in his autobiography, "Suddenly, I — the Editor of the Emporia *Gazette* — a country paper with little more than five hundred circulation, was a somebody. The dimensions of my world were enlarged."

Within months, as the name William Allen White still echoed around the country, his book *The Real Issue* hit the stores. This collection of Kansas stories, published in fall 1896, was hailed by reviewers. *Life* magazine noted, "It is a pleasure to find that Mr. White has just as original ideas about story writing as he has exhibited in editorials." Popular magazines of the day, such as *McClure's*, began requesting permission to reprint stories from the book and paid $500 per story! The book also took Will east of the Mississippi River for the first time. Visiting his publisher in Chicago, Will met famous authors such as Hamlin Garland, dined in fancy restaurants and toured his publisher's home, which was designed by Frank Lloyd Wright. All that thrilled Will, but he did not forget his roots.

"I was always conscious of the Walnut Creek water and never pretended I had

The Populist Party

Also known as "The People's Party," this political party annoyed William Allen White even in his El Dorado newspaper days. By the time he moved to the *Gazette*, its influence was growing beyond the midwest.

Populism appealed to those who considered themselves common people, especially farmers. Populists typically displayed a distrust or resentment of wealth. William Allen White, who wore suits as fancy as he could afford and didn't hide his wide-ranging knowledge, made a perfect target for populists in El Dorado and, later, Emporia.

Will was not afraid to voice his disgust with the party, especially once he got his own newspaper. In 1891, an El Dorado Populist parade included a dummy in a nice suit with "Silly Willie" written across the seat of the pants. In 1896, still wearing nice suits, "Willie" remained the target of teasing Populists—only this time their teasing pushed their target to national fame when he dashed off "What's the Matter with Kansas?"

any other kind of steam in my pipes," he recalled. Nevertheless, it was then that he began to lead what he called a double life — running a small Kansas newspaper, but also traveling far beyond his state's boundaries to conduct business and make speeches.

After the success of "What's the Matter with Kansas?" Will for the second time met the president of the United States, William McKinley. At a political celebration in Ohio, Will asked the president's campaign manager, Mark Hanna, for a letter of introduction — one

William McKinley

stating he wanted no political office — and it worked. With one exception, that was a principle Will adhered to his entire life. Despite his fascination with the political scene, he preferred to remain an onlooker, free to comment on things as he saw them.

The Whites soon traveled to Washington, D.C., to discuss the appointment of a postmaster in Emporia. There they met a man who was to become a great friend to the nation as well as the Whites — Theodore Roosevelt. In 1897 Roosevelt was working for the Department of the Navy and requested a meeting with Will. He had read *The Real Issue* and some of Will's editorials. At lunch, the two talked for an hour and a half. Recalling it, White wrote, "I had never known such a man as he, and never shall again."

On that same trip, Will used his railroad pass to

Theodore Roosevelt in his Rough Rider garb, not many years after he met William Allen White.

27

A new building for the Gazette *on Merchant Street, which needed paving.*

travel to New York to visit the office of *McClure's Magazine*. There he met renowned authors such as William Dean Howells and Ida Tarbell. They became lifelong friends and supporters of White.

The influence of these powerful people boosted Will's status in political and literary circles around the United States. It also helped financially. Before that year was over, he won a big government printing job for the *Gazette*. With the sizable income from that, from the stories and articles he was publishing in national magazines, and from an offer for another book of Kansas stories (*The Court of Boyville*), Will was able to buy a new printing press and pay off the original loan that helped him buy the *Gazette*. All this happened by the time he turned 30. Plans soon began for a new building for the newspaper.

Things improved at home, too. In July 1899, Will and Sallie moved into a 10-room Queen Anne Victorian style home at 927 Exchange St. It was built in 1885 for a lawyer, and because of the red bricks and red sandstone used in its construction, it was called Red Rocks.

The house provided a perfect base for the double life Will and Sallie would lead the

The Whites' permanent home for more than four decades, known by Emporians as Red Rocks.

rest of their lives. The Whites rented it and set to work modernizing it. Like their previous home, it had no electricity, running water or natural gas service.

Nevertheless, Red Rocks provided no end of pleasure. As Will recalled in his autobiography: "We used to walk up and down the sidewalk in the summer twilight admiring it with 'wonder, awe and praise'. Here we have lived ever since. Here our children were born. Here we have seen the major pageant of our lives pass. Here we have lived, indeed, happily ever after."

Despite all his visits around the country, Will did not ignore his hometown. He was a booster who delighted in celebrating Emporia in his editorials. In 1899 he led a group of merchants who instituted a three-day street fair. It aimed to increase pride in the city as well as to increase business. Word spread about the fair, which took place September 18 to 20, 1899, and White arranged for excursion trains to bring people from around the state. There were parades, a baby show, Indian dancers, a cakewalk and entertainment under a big circus tent. The highlight of the festival was the drive down Emporia's main street of "the first car seen west of the Mississippi".

By the turn of the century, Will was a proud homeowner, a famous author (working on his third book), a politically active Republican — and a father.

William Lindsay White was born June 17, 1900, weighing 10 pounds and keeping his father home from the Republican National Convention that year. In an

One of Emporia's turn-of-the-century street fairs, a favorite local cause for William Allen White.

All dressed up for a relaxed portrait on the porch of Red Rocks.

editorial six days later, Will suggested that his son be called Bill.

Describing himself at the time he became a father, Will said he possessed "...brown hair, a complexion that sunburned easily, large blue eyes, a big mouth wherein baby teeth never were replaced, giving it a snaggle-toothed appearance, a long neck capped by two double chins...I was just a fat slob who was trying to hide, under the exuberance of youth...my obvious short-comings...In the summer I bedecked myself in white...I must have looked like a skinned elephant."

Willingness to make himself part of the joke would win Will many friends and much influence in years to come.

Chapter Four

Finding the Center

*a*s the new century began, Will's involvement in national politics grew along with his friendship with Theodore Roosevelt. When Roosevelt returned as a hero from the Spanish-American War and was elected governor of New York, he and Will began an exchange of letters that continued the rest of Roosevelt's life.

Will shared his belief that Roosevelt could someday be president, and said so in *Gazette* editorials. When Roosevelt was elected vice president in 1900, Will began to organize Republicans around the country to nominate him for president in 1904. Will was his chief organizer in Kansas, and was thrilled to ride with Roosevelt on a train that carried the vice president through several states as he laid plans to run for president.

When the train stopped at stations, Roosevelt spoke to crowds from the platform at the back. In Emporia, he stepped off the train to greet Sallie and little Bill White. It was the first of several visits he would make to Emporia, and Will visited him at his home in Oyster Bay, N.Y., as well. "Teddy" once brought a jaguar rug as a gift for Bill, and Bill reciprocated by naming his fox terrier after him. Will's prediction of a presidency for Roosevelt came

The jaguar rug that Theodore Roosevelt gave young Bill White.

true more quickly than expected. On September 6, 1901, an assassin shot President McKinley, who died a week later. That made Theodore Roosevelt president.

On the night before Roosevelt was to move into the White House, Will visited him as he would many times through the rest of Roosevelt's tenure. His friendship with the president did much to cement his reputation around the world, and Will began to receive offers of full-time work from New York magazines.

After receiving an offer of $8,000 a year from one publisher, Will wrote a friend: "...I could not go out of Kansas for eight thousand or ten thousand or twice ten thousand. It is not a question of money that keeps me in Kansas.

"Writing with me is not altogether a matter of money," he continued. "I really want to do honest work. To do that work, I have to write about the things that interest me....the *Gazette* and Emporia furnish me that recreation and life that I like. They give me an independence that money could not buy."

William Allen White began many a journey from the Santa Fe station in Emporia.

For years to come, Will wrote to potential employers many such letters with basically the same theme.

His friend, author Dorothy Canfield Fisher, later observed: "It has been assumed that the small-town man would shake the provincial dust from his feet as soon as a good chance offered, and go to live in some great center. 'Center of what?' the Whites asked the world with a mocking laugh, settling down to stay where they belonged. For them the center was where they could share most deeply

THE EMPORIA GAZETTE.

VOL. II.   EMPORIA, KANSAS, TUESDAY, EVENING, FEBRUARY 5, 1901.   NUMBER

Terry up for Ravens.

Fire Boss dour is the best.

Dr. Gray, Dentist, 14 West Sixth.

Mrs. J. G Hutchinson is much better.

A good mine may be found at 1106

Dr. Metcalf, of Osby, was in town yesterday.

If you have that tired feeling, smoke our Knocker.

A Calm Dissertation.

In his sermon on Carrie Nation Sunday night which is the talk of the town this week—Rev. Madison, pastor of the First Methodist church laid great stress upon the wisdom of calmness in discussing the matter. Whenever he came to a particularly striking climax in his remarks he was careful to add that he was perfectly calm. He opened his discourse by saying that certain politicians don't like to see preachers in politics. Then

powers in attacking a woman. For just the moment you put any restriction on the saloon keeper, you can be sure he will be an outlaw within twenty-four hours, because he will not pay any attention to it unless he has to. You put a local option upon him and he will break the conditions of it. You seek to control the saloon by a low license and he will break the law about it. You put on a high license and he will transgress the terms of it. And then, of course, if you undertake to prohibit you will have

great importance of their seeing it that, when they determine how their ballots shall be cast, that they do it with reference to this question as well as to others. You must determine where best your vote shall go, other man, private or public, a right to urge that the great principles and the great questions, and all of them, be considered when you make up your minds. Again I repeat that we are to bear our responsibility in this thing. I, myself, hope for a great revolution

AWFUL CONDITIONS EXIST.

The Famine in China Has Driven Natives to the Extremity of Eating Human Flesh.

BITTER COLD ADDS TO THE MISERY.

Parents Are Dying Insane by the Car

KANSAS LEGISLATURE.

Bill for Convict Labor on Public Roads Is Senate—House to Draft a New Text-Book Bill

Topeka, Kan., Feb. 5.—The senate, after a rest of three days, convened at four p. m. yesterday for a short session. Henley, of Douglas, introduced a bill providing for convict labor on the public roads.

Vincent introduced a resolution instructing the attorney general to begin a suit in the federal court to prevent the state of Colorado from di-

IN HONOR OF MA

One Hundredth Annivers Installation of the First C tice Appropriately Obs

EXERCISES AT THE NATIONAL

In the Hall of the House of

The owner's name, proudly inscribed on the Gazette *building in Emporia.*

in human life. Our modern world was for them not a long table, but a round one. There is no head or foot to it. So why move? They never did."

Will found he could purchase Red Rocks for $6,000, and was able to do so borrowing money from the publisher of *McClure's* magazine. The money he had borrowed from a local bank to build a new building for the *Gazette* was paid back by June 1901. He saw publication of his third book, a collection of political articles previously published in magazines entitled *Stratagems and Spoils*. Meanwhile, little Bill turned 1 year old, having spent hours of his babyhood in a basket beside his mother's desk in the *Gazette* office as she worked on her society column.

By the end of 1901, long days at the *Gazette* followed by late nights at home working on magazine articles — as well as train travel back and forth from Emporia — caught up with Will. His doctors ordered a vacation. Leaving young Bill in the care of his two grandmothers and the *Gazette* in the capable hands of its strong managing editor and staff, he and Sallie went to Catalina Island off the coast of California.

They stayed away until May 1902, and the vacation became a pattern through the rest of Will's life. He would work himself into what doctors called "nervous exhaustion," and then leave Emporia for a month or more to relax. During his absences, of course, the letters and the telegrams flew, and the mail brought the *Gazette* each day.

These periodic forced vacations became part of the double life that Will led.

Chapter Five

Around the World

In his middle 30s, Will delighted in politics, writing, travel and family life. He could call the President of the United States a firm friend, he had published four books and he was still writing articles for national magazines.

On June 18, 1904, when Will was 36, he became a father once again. This time brought a daughter, Mary Katherine, named for Will's mother.

Mary was a handful and always would be. When Mary was three months old, Sallie wrote little Bill, who was visiting Colorado with his grandmother, that the infant "still yells loud and long and is a pretty bad girl."

"She won't sleep at all without someone sits and rocks her," Sallie continued, "and then she wakes up and looks around and laughs at everybody as if she thought she was an awful good girl.

"She is growing up to be such a pretty girl and her eyes are just like yours and she is twice as bad

Facing page: Dad took it on the nose from son. Above: A few years older and less cantankerous, young Bill posed with his mother and the White family's newest addition, Mary.

about her nurses as you used to be."

As a baby, Mary was sickly. To give her the benefit of cool mountain air, the Whites began spending whole summers in Colorado in a rented cabin near Pike's

Will's mother lived here, next door to the Whites' home.

Peak. To keep in touch with the *Gazette*, Will took the train back and forth from Colorado Springs to Emporia and also used the telegraph office. He wrote a series of short stories based on his early years in the newspaper business. *The Saturday Evening Post* magazine paid handsomely for them, nearly $2,500 for one story.

Before Mary turned a year old, a red brick home was built for Will's mother just south of Red Rocks. "Madam White," as Will's mother was called, still joined her son and his family for dinner and often brought Will's favorite foods. Meanwhile, the Whites hired a housekeeper to live with them to cook and clean.

They also bought a horse and buggy. The event found its way into the *Gazette* in 1906:

"The editor of this paper desires to buy a horse. He and his family have reached a point in social prominence and affluence where they feel that they can afford to drive out of a summer evening and look at other people's porch boxes, and admire other people's flower gardens.... The animal also should be gentle, and of the kind that children can use to teeter-totter across."

They paid $125 for the horse and named him Old Tom. The buggy cost $325 and had a canopy edged in fringe. The horse and buggy served the Whites for many years, even after cars began to fill Emporia's streets.

Will's memoirs about his early years in journalism were published in 1905 in a book called *In Our Town*. One day, a letter arrived from a fellow author, Mark

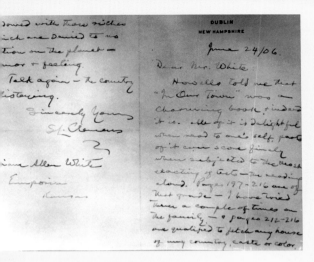

DUBLIN
NEW HAMPSHIRE

June 24/06.

Dear Mr. White:

Heady compliments from America's most famous writer.

Twain, who complimented the book and encouraged Will, "Talk again, the country is listening."

Will and Sallie, ever partners, discussed writing something longer than editorials and short stories. In February 1905 work began on a novel based on the Bible's story of the prodigal son but set in modern times. Will worked on it when he had time in Emporia and took his typewriter on summer vacations to Colorado. Little did the Whites know it would take four rewrites and four years before the world would read and appreciate *A Certain Rich Man.*

Meanwhile, the *Gazette* benefited from Will's success outside Emporia. By 1905 the newspaper was printed on the latest of presses. Type was no longer set by hand, one metal character at a time. Instead the paper installed two keyboard-operated Linotype machines. Two more Linotypes were added in 1907.

Linotype typesetting machines made printers' work easier and faster, although Will never learned to operate them. This one remains on display at the Gazette.

One of William Allen White's typewriters.

"When I walked into that office in 1895," Will recalled, "I could do everything that I asked anyone else to do. I had swept floors. I had set type. I had made up the type in forms. I had put it on the press and had fed the press.... Ten years later, when I walked over the threshold of the mechanical room of the *Gazette*, I could not do one process that led from the copy desk to the printed page."

One thing did not change at the *Gazette*. Will's office remained in the center of the building. It still housed his old rolltop desk and the doors still were open

to the staff at all times. Observed former *Gazette* reporter Rolla A. Clymer, "Even the humblest and least important workers about the office were made to feel that they were associates and partners in a worthy enterprise — not just payroll units."

Will's friendship with President Roosevelt made him a confidante of many other political figures. He traveled from Emporia to state and national capitals attending meetings as well as reporting on politics.

As Roosevelt finished his second term in 1909, he invited the Whites to a final party in the White House. The evening ended with Will and the President talking by the fireplace in the Roosevelt family's private quarters. Years would pass before Will again had such access to a president.

Shortly after the Whites returned from Washington, they began preparing for their first trip to Europe. They had been saving for 10 years to take it, and it was to be a family voyage. Bill, going on 9 years old, and Mary, now 5, accompanied them. So did Will's mother, who was in her 70s.

In those days, the only way to cross the Atlantic Ocean was by ship. Will did not fare well at sea.

"I saw more of the pattern of springs above me in Mary's berth than I saw of the bounding billows," he remembered — and little Mary sometimes wet the bed. In more than 10 subsequent trips abroad, seasickness was his constant companion in the early days of each voyage. Once his stomach adjusted to its new surroundings, however, he enjoyed walking the deck with Sallie and visiting people on board.

In Europe, the Whites met famous people wherever they went, in keeping

Facing page: An influential visitor to Red Rocks, Theodore Roosevelt, stood with Will, young Bill and friends.

with Will's renown. The new President of the United States, William Howard Taft, gave the Whites a letter of introduction. He wrote, "...Mr. White is a journalist of national reputation, and a warm friend of mine."

In Rome they met the pope. In England they met authors Thomas Hardy and Henry James. They saw all the sights and in Rome stayed a week at a hotel with marble floors and two fountains in the courtyard. The bill for five people, including three meals a day, was only $31.

Memorable experiences happened aboard ship, too. One morning on deck, Will glanced at a New York newspaper that a passenger was reading. He caught sight of his name in an advertisement. Borrowing the paper, Will found that the ad was for his first book of fiction, *A Certain Rich Man*, and that it was already in its fourth printing! In the privacy of their cabin, the family celebrated and said a prayer of thanks for another success.

Upon their return to the United States, the Whites were greeted at the dock in New York City by a crowd of friends from the publishing world. The real surprise, however, awaited when the family got off the train in Emporia.

"Any Emporian's trip to Europe was a matter of town-wide interest," Will remembered in his autobiography. Nevertheless, news of his book's great success created more than the usual excitement. Townspeople, some dressed as characters from *A Certain Rich Man*, turned out to greet their world-famous author in a well-planned celebration. A banner stretched

Fliers advertised Will's first fiction book, which proved to be a hit.

A big homecoming welcome was staged in Emporia for Will and family.

across the street, a band played, and friends from around Kansas were on hand.

A band followed the carriage as it headed for Red Rocks, drawn as usual by Old Tom. On arrival, the band played "Home Sweet Home." If Will ever doubted his decision to stay in Emporia, that outpouring of appreciation surely affirmed it for him and his family.

Chapter Six

No Place Like Home

"**P**eople run all over the world looking for beauty, and the truth is only they who stay at home find it," William Allen White wrote in the *Gazette* on April 26, 1901. The home he and Sallie created at Red Rocks became a cradle for their children, an oasis for their famous visiting friends and a haven for them.

From the time they moved in as renters in 1899, the house began to evolve to fit their lifestyle. Flower gardens and a lily pond made the back yard a pleasant place to entertain and an east upstairs room became a study for Will. The third floor made an ideal playroom for Bill and Mary and their neighborhood friends on rainy days.

Red Rocks won local renown for parties each Christmas for neighborhood children and the staff of the *Gazette*, caramel apples at Halloween and an ever-ready guest room.

Jane Addams, known nationwide as a crusader on behalf of immigrants and the poor, visited at Red Rocks in 1908. Author Edna Ferber took advantage of the guest room often. She wrote in her autobiography, "When your world is awry and hope dead and vitality low and the appetite gone there is no ocean trip, no month in the country, no known drug equal to the reviving quality of twenty-four hours

Dinner on the lawn of Red Rocks. This one honored Herbert Hoover.

spent on the front porch or in the sitting room of the Whites' house in Emporia.

"Practically everyone of any importance in America has at one time or another stopped at the White house on their way East or West. Myself, I've been known to take a sneaking trip to Colorado or California just as an excuse for stopping over. There are hundreds of stories about the Whites' hospitality, and they're all true."

Red Rocks stood on the edge of Stringtown, a neighborhood where many of Emporia's lower-income black residents lived. On other sides it was adjoined by neighborhoods of homes owned by lower- and middle-income white residents. The Whites never moved to an area where neighbors' wealth would match their own.

Century School

They simply lived the life they chose and didn't worry that they were the only family in the neighborhood that hosted famous guests, traveled to Europe, employed a "hired girl," or owned fine china, silver, a piano and even a Victrola, an early-day record player.

In fact, the Whites' generosity was well-known. When a neighbor across the street suffered a stroke, Sallie and Will assured family members that food, coal and kindling for the fire would be provided. They insisted that the child of the house join Bill and Mary at Red Rocks to play each day. Decades later, that little girl recounted the incident.

A young *Gazette* employee remembered a delightful evening at Red Rocks, leaving with a gift of books from the White's library. When the same employee moved to a larger home months later, a van sent by Sallie White brought rugs, a coffee table and several chairs no longer needed in her home.

The little girl who lived across the street also recalled how the unelected "mayor" of Stringtown often sat on the porch of Red Rocks and discussed neighborhood problems. Will promised to use his influence and share those concerns with city officials. Toward the end of Will's life, a national magazine observed: "Come to dinner with Will and Sallie White, who might have traveled with prince and potentate but chose instead to stay at home and be plain people."

Bill and Mary attended Century School with other neighborhood children, black and white. Morning walks to school down 10th Avenue were joined by black children from the neighborhood. Years later, Bill recalled at least one birthday party invitation that included several black playmates.

Red Rocks provided a base from which Bill and his sister Mary roamed the neighborhood. Sallie thought it was important for her children to dress comfortably and get plenty of physical activity. They joined other children in games of hide-and-seek or pretend battles and put on shows in a neighbor's tent charging a button for attendance. Once, Will asked city workers to dump a large pile of sand in his home's backyard for the children to enjoy. Forts, a Great Wall of China, Roman cities and battlegrounds emerged before the sand ran its course. "It was a curious kind of Disneyland," Bill remembered.

One of Bill's dogs and Mary's burro usually joined the fun. More than once a board was placed on the burro's back to make a teeter-totter! Swimming and canoeing in the river were favorite summertime activities, and frogs, toads and tadpoles sometimes made their way back to the Red Rocks playroom. When Bill and his friends skinny-dipped, Mary wore her summertime uniform — overalls.

On the surface, Will and Sallie's children appeared

Barefoot and dressed comfortably, Bill and Mary were ready for play.

Cleaned up and posed for the studio camera, Bill and Mary survived the photo session.

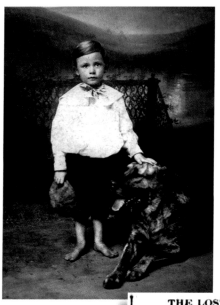

Animals all around: In an early hint at her lifelong love of riding, Mary sat atop a small mule. An unidentified youth, perhaps the handler of the animal, stood next to her. For young Bill, a dog made a friendly photo prop.

opposite in temperament.

Mary "was the spark plug who kept the wheels going around in our neighborhood," the Whites' little neighbor remembered. "Small and fragile-looking as she was, she had a foghorn voice and it often could be heard booming up and down the block."

Bill didn't call attention to himself but loved pranks, no doubt appreciated by his mischievous sister. Sometimes, he caught lightning bugs in a jar and set them loose in the room he shared with Mary. Bill's friend Cecil

This article in the Gazette seeking a lost dog was unsigned, but obviously the work of Will. Young Bill's dog, Teddy, was missing.

LOST.

A dog—a little, white fox terrier with liver colored ears, and dark intelligent eyes; an oldish dog as dogs go, being past 12, and slow moving, a bit deaf and may-be not so clear sighted as he was once when two little children used to tumble him over the grass at his home 10 years ago. He has always been a good mor-al dog, and if he had his love af-fairs, and romantic adventures he was always in by 9 o'clock. But now he has been gone two days. Possibly he has been crippled in an accident; it is also possible that he is sick, and it is barely possible that he may have gone to a home where there are children, though such perfidy seems unlike-ly. But at any rate anyone who knows of such a dog who left home Sunday morning will please call up phone 28 and tell the news be it good or bad to an anxious family to whom the little dog is a living link to a happy and beauti-ful past.

THE LOST IS FOUND.

For five days the Gazette t phone has been ringing to tell editor of people who thought t had found his little lost dog. seems to have been raining w fox terriers of a certain age w stumped tails and yellow e in and around Emporia. none of the dogs descri over the phone was the real l dog except one—and he was dog we long had sought mourned because we found l not. C. W. Jacobs found him y terday morning 10 miles east town just north of the Sixth enue road. The dog was lying a wisp of hay in the road—star and sad and footsore. How he come there no one knows; whe er he had followed off wine, we en or song, or had been kidnap by people who turned him lo when they realized what an dog he was—that no one can s But the Jacobs family took h gave him food and a place beh the kitchen stove, and phoned his people.

From all over the country ters and telegrams have come response to the notice that this tle dog was lost. Nothing in world, excepting a child will dr people together in sympathy the love of dogs.

Rowboats at the ready on the Cottonwood River at Emporia. Young Bill, above right, with pal Cecil Carle and pet mouse.

Carle remembered collecting June bugs in a matchbox to hide under Mary's bed. The bugs would "...dive bomb the room once the light was turned on," Carle said.

Both children inherited their parents' love of books and did not need to look outside Red Rocks if they wanted one. A neighbor remembered: "There were oceans of books — almost as many as in the city library. The finest-looking books were in the big parlor behind glass doors in cases across from the fireplace. The long hall on the second floor was lined with shelves of books, books were everywhere in Will's study and even the playroom had books on two walls. In no other house had I seen half as many books.... In scores of books at Red Rocks I found autographs expressing the writer's high regard for Will White."

According to the neighbor, Bill and Mary often were bored in school — and sometimes knew more than the teacher — because of their "incessant reading, from travel, from exposure to the talk of brilliant people." Listening to their parents added to their education as well. Bill remembered, "They

Part of the Whites' ocean of books.

Will and Sallie, together as always.

talked things over every night; we could hear it all coming up the stairwell over the banisters."

One of the things Will liked about his home was its proximity to the center of town. Much of his working life, he walked the eight or so blocks to work at the *Gazette*. As he walked, he visited with people in their yards and noticed his surroundings, things that often found their way into his editorials.

"When a house is adorned by garden flowers," he wrote, "it is a sign that someone in the house, perhaps every one in the house, is trying to give pleasure to the neighbors and passing strangers."

His walk began each morning with a ritual that fascinated his little across-the-street neighbor:

"After breakfast at Red Rocks Will and Sallie White would come down the wide steps of the castle, on to the sidewalk, and turn south toward downtown. When they were about half way to the corner of Exchange Street and Ninth Avenue, I would edge out the front door to get a better look. Will would stride along with his briefcase under his arm. Sallie would have difficulty keeping step — matching her tiny feet to Will's pudgy ones.

"At the corner, Will would lean his briefcase against an elm tree, draw Sallie to his rotund front and give her a smacking kiss. I watched in amazement. Emporia men did not kiss their wives on street corners when I was young."

Fireplace in the parlor at Red Rocks.

About Red Rocks, *Gazette* employee Ruth Garver Gagliardo had a theory: "...to be in their home, I discovered, was to experience a deep sense of leisure — the pressures were off. This mastery over time which both of them had in marked degree, may explain in great part the immense amount of work Mr. White was able to turn out."

It certainly helps explain the charm of Red Rocks, which drew the famous and the local and nourished the White family, always awaiting them on their return from their journeys.

Great Adventures

*W*ill's first book of fiction sold 25,000 copies in the first five months after its publication in 1909, and the money raised from that was turned toward improvements at the *Gazette*.

Afterward, Will began work on a series of articles about the national political scene. *The Old Order Changeth*, a collection of those articles, came out in 1910, the same year Theodore Roosevelt visited Kansas to dedicate a memorial to abolitionist John Brown.

Will's relationship with the former president grew closer as the years went by, and in 1912 he helped form a third political party to assist in Roosevelt's campaign for another term as president. The party was formally known as the Progressive Party, but came to be called the Bull Moose party. That name came from Roosevelt's reply to a reporter's question about how he felt upon arriving for the Republican National Convention that year:

Uncashed check from Will's publisher. Below, ticket to the Progressive Convention of 1912.

September 1912: Campaigning in Kansas, Theodore Roosevelt visited Red Rocks, this time with his assistant, cousin Emlen Roosevelt. The dog on Bill's lap was Teddy.

"Like a bull moose!"

Roosevelt toured the country by train early in the campaign and again visited Emporia in September 1912. A tour of Emporia in the carriage with Old Tom, a dinner of fried chicken, mashed potatoes and creamed gravy after church, an hour-long nap and stimulating conversation provided a much-needed break from campaigning for Roosevelt and a major break from the ordinary for the town of Emporia.

The Whites' dining room as it looks today.

Quite used to famous guests, that day Mary chose to eat in the kitchen, where she, Bill and a neighbor child witnessed an incident no one in the dining room suspected. As the Whites' cook and housekeeper rushed around the kitchen putting the finishing touches on the meal that would be served to Roosevelt, the steaming platter of golden fried chicken slid off the oven top and onto the floor. The practical woman quickly picked up every piece, washed and reheated the platter and piled the chicken back on it.

"I washed this kitchen floor this morning," she told the wide-eyed children. "If any of you tell Sallie White about this, I'll murder you. She has enough on her mind. No use worrying her with what can't be helped." The platter made its way out to the dining room table, where Roosevelt enjoyed three pieces of fried chicken and bragged for years to come about its quality.

The next day, Will commented in the *Gazette*: "The people of Emporia treated Theodore Roosevelt with the greatest kindness and consideration yesterday. They left him absolutely alone, as his hosts asked the town to do.... Manners are only good morals in better things, and Emporia's kind heart never was shown more clearly than yesterday when the town gave a tired man an opportunity for complete rest." Despite the hard work of Will and others, Roosevelt lost the election to Woodrow Wilson, and, within four years, the Bull Moose Party lost its support as well.

Author Edna Ferber met Will for the first time at the 1912

Will as a proud homeowner in 1909.

Republican National Convention in Chicago and felt an immediate bond. Her description of their meeting provides a glimpse of Will's appearance and attitude at that time: "I saw a rotund broad-shouldered man in a pale gray suit and astonishing pale gray kid shoes that he displayed with pride as having been snared from a shoe drummer in Emporia, Kansas...He had the smile of a roguish little boy, with dimples complete; the broad noble brow of a philosopher and statesman; the eyes of a poet and the shrewd determined mouth of the politician, businessman, newspaper editor. The eyes dominated. I noticed that ordinarily they were a rather washed-out blue as though the color had drained out of them when he relaxed. When he was stirred, emotionalized, they would darken and deepen and widen until they were blue-black pools in his round pink face...We were friends and comrades from the start."

Will in 1912.

In the midst of Will's greatest political involvement in 1912, he had also begun another book of fiction called *In the Heart of a Fool*, which he would work on between other projects for the next seven years. That same summer, counting on money he'd be paid for covering the national conventions, the Whites bought a cabin on a hillside in Moraine Park, Colorado, with a spectacular view of the mountain Will climbed as a young man, Longs Peak. While he had time for only one week there that summer, he would later write, "...it was to be for all our lives a haven and a refuge."

The Whites were able to spend time away from Emporia because of the outstanding staff they had assembled over the years. So many young reporters spent their early career at the *Gazette* that it became known as the "Gazette School of Journalism" and many of them went on to great success. Cal Lambert, later *Gazette* city editor, remembered, "No employee who ever worked for the *Gazette* left Mr. White's service without love and affection for him. No school of journalism could compete with a job on the

Will's summertime writing cabin at Moraine Park in the Colorado Rockies.

Emporia poet and Gazette *staff member Walt Mason.*

Gazette." The *Gazette's* original printer's devil, or helper, Walter Hughes, became Will's trusted business manager until his death in 1932. Laura French, who joined the staff shortly after Will arrived, worked her way up to city editor, a job she held for 16 years. In 1911, her style rules for the *Gazette* were committed to print. "Tell your story in the first sentence, then follow with details," she wisely advised, but also warned, "Don't use Mr. White's name — say 'the *Gazette*', or cut it out altogether if you can't say "the *Gazette*'. You might lose your job otherwise." Poet Walt Mason provided copy for nearly 15 years and went on to fame on his own. Sallie herself sometimes took charge when Will alone was out of town. The *Gazette* even had its own city-league baseball team.

After the election of 1912, the White family needed a major vacation. This time, they rented a beach house in La Jolla, California, for four months. While the children played in the Pacific Ocean under

They were the champs: the Gazette-sponsored baseball team in 1910.

the watchful eye of their Grandma White and the maid, Will and Sallie completely rewrote the novel, read newspapers from around the country — including the *Gazette*, of course — and current magazines, many featuring Will's stories.

They returned to find business booming on the *Gazette* and another linotype machine needed. By this time, more and more automobiles were showing up on Emporia's few paved streets. Will traded $1,300 worth of advertising with an auto dealer for a car, a Chandler. When the dealer's son delivered the car to the *Gazette* with instructions to include a driving lesson, Will invited several employees to accompany him. The lesson did not go well. Will ended up in a front yard north of town. He decided that he preferred the carriage ride behind Old Tom and sold the car to a doctor in a neighboring town.

At his Colorado retreat, a rustic table held Will's typewriter and piles of paper.

In summer, the Whites spent more time at their cabin in Colorado. In fact, they had built a 14-foot porch using native stone on three sides of the main cabin and added a work cabin for Will and two small sleeping cabins for the children or visitors. Will moved his typewriter into the smaller cabin and spent hours working on his novel.

Across the road, the Big Thompson River rushed along, and young Bill developed a talent for catching trout, which his father cooked over the cabin's fire.

Back in 1889, when as a college student Will spent the summer in Colorado, he had pitched in with chores and joined in activities. However, as an adult Will never hiked, fished, or chopped wood for the fireplace. When he wasn't typing, he was relaxing in a hammock swung across the front porch of the cabin. Mary spent her time doing crafts and tending the mules at the nearby YMCA camp.

Trips to their Colorado retreat eventually ceased to be by train. By 1915, possibly with pressure from Bill and Mary, the Whites purchased the first car they would keep. Again it was paid for partly by advertising in the *Gazette*. The 750-mile drive between Emporia and the Colorado cabin took three days; the dirt roads common in those days sometimes were washed out by rain.

Driving was another thing Will would not do. As an adult, Bill shared memories of trying to teach his father to drive:

"I put him behind the wheel, showed him the starter button, the clutch, the gear shift and the brake, all of which he seemed to understand, and then showed him how to twist the steering wheel to turn a corner. So then he pressed the starter button, shifted gears according to the lesson, and we began to roll. Presently we came to a corner. Again, according to the lesson, he cramped the steering wheel.

Auto Road in Denver Mountain Parks, between Golden and Idaho Springs.

"The car turned, but he did not seem to realize there could be any need to turn the steering wheel back. So we kept on turning, jumping the curbing and ended up against an elm tree on a neighbor's lawn, which didn't greatly matter because I had managed to get my foot on the brake." His attempts at driving evidently never leaving his mind, Will engaged Bill or Sallie and later Mary or the cook to drive him places.

In February that same year, Will began discussions with an important architect named Frank Lloyd Wright on remodeling Red Rocks. Wright had designed the Chicago home of Will's publisher Chauncey Williams in 1895, not to mention scores of other buildings in Chicago and elsewhere that won Wright international attention. His work was bold and unconventional, and he had a well-known ego and temper.

In his reply to Will's first letter, Wright cautioned him that big changes might be necessary: "The house might pass away under the aesthetics [meaning "anesthetics"] of the necessary surgical operation, but if you can face that possibility calmly, I can and will do my best." Will and Sallie decided they could face that possibility and sent Wright a "wish list" of desired changes. Dormer windows upstairs, a coal stove in the kitchen and a porch roof "like a trellis" were included.

Letters and telegrams flew between the Whites and the architect as plans were drawn up. Wright continued to see the activity as a life-saving surgery for the old house, while Will feared it would become unrecognizable. Also, he balked at the $10,000 price tag (Wright's jobs included furnishings as well).

Will's friend Henry J. Allen had no such fear. By August 1916, plans were well under way for a stylish Frank Lloyd Wright home for his family in Wichita

"Allen's home will be an 'oasis' in the architectural desert of Kansas," Wright wrote in an August 25, 1916, letter to Will, "and I am anxious to get you into an 'atmosphere' that is worthy of you."

Evidently, the Whites kept balking at Wright's ideas. By September of that year, a frustrated Wright exclaimed: "Get reckless. Have the real-thing, when it can be found, no matter what it costs — it's the only thing that's not cheap."

Eventually, Wright suggested to Will a more traditional firm, Wight & Wight of Kansas City, and plans for the remodeling were completed, retaining some of Frank Lloyd Wright's ideas.

Famous friends: Early conservationist Gifford Pinchot, left, talked to a distinguished audience including Gutzon Borglum, sculptor of Mount Rushmore, and a cowboy-hatted Will White. The woman was probably Will's fellow author, Willa Cather.

When work on his second novel grew difficult, Will wrote articles or short stories. *God's Puppets*, another collection of stories, came out in 1916, keeping the name of William Allen White alive in literary circles of the day. Again that year, Will was active in national politics. In its second national campaign, the Bull Moose Progressives nominated Theodore Roosevelt for president, only to see him turn down the nomination at the convention.

Will, who brought teenaged Bill to the convention, commented later that the four years spent with the Bull Moose Party was "...a great adventure, politically and emotionally probably the greatest adventure of my life." In future years, Will dedicated himself more to state politics, although he continued to cover both Democratic and Republican national conventions most of the rest of his life.

Chapter Eight

Leaving Youth Behind

*W*oodrow Wilson was re-elected president in 1916 on the motto "he kept us out of war." However, he was unable to keep that promise very long after his inauguration. In April 1917, he asked Congress to declare war on Germany, and the United States entered the first World War.

William Allen White disliked the new president personally, and he wrote editorials warning of the folly of war. Once the United States entered the war in Europe, however, Will did all he could to support the effort. He headed money-raising campaigns and wrote thought-provoking editorials.

On April 13, 1917, he reminded readers, "We should all remember during the present hostilities that the present war is between the American people and the German government, and not between the American people and the German people." In the face of widespread anti-German sentiment, he urged people to continue to listen to music by German composers, read books by German authors and be ready to accept Germany once the war was over.

In an editorial published March 5, 1918, Will praised the children of a local couple who raised two Shetland ponies and donated them to the Red Cross to be

Facing page: On a Red Cross visit to the battlefields in France, Will joked with a French soldier and with his Kansas friend, Henry Allen.

sold for the war effort. He wrote from experience as a fundraiser for the Red Cross.

The previous summer and fall, 49-year-old Will and his long-time friend Henry Allen visited France as inspectors for the Red Cross. Every day he wrote home describing the conditions of both the soldiers and the French people. When he returned to Kansas, Sallie insisted he gather the letters she had kept into a book. As he described *The Martial Adventures of Henry and Me*, published in 1918, it was "the story of two fat middle-aged men who went to war without their wives." The trip also provided Will subject matter for several magazine articles.

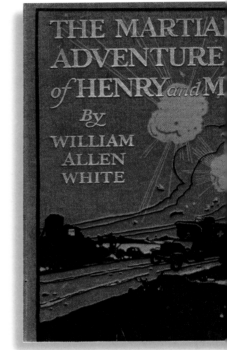

Revising his novel *In the Heart of a Fool* for the fourth time and seeing it published, entertaining famous visitors at his home, receiving honorary degrees at various universities, promoting the candidacy for governor of his friend Henry Allen and overseeing further growth of the *Gazette* led Will into his 50th year. To celebrate that milestone birthday, Sallie organized a dinner party at Red Rocks.

Before the guests arrived, Will found himself "... sitting down midway on the stairway landing and bursting into tears. To be fifty was definitely to leave youth, and young manhood, and to begin to be an old man."

In December 1918 the "old man" traveled again to France, this time with 18-year-old Bill, to report on the peace conference that would end the World War and to serve as a representative of the Red Cross. Before their ship sailed from New York, they visited Theodore Roosevelt, very ill in the hospital. News of his death reached them after only three days in Paris.

"Not since my father's death had grief stabbed me so poignantly as those headlines cut into my heart that gray, cold Paris morning," Will wrote later.

He poured himself into work at the crowded conference but also took time to meet with friends who were there. He and Bill toured Germany and England before his return home. As he had done on his 1917 trip to France, Will paid his own expenses.

"In politics, a man must pay for his freedom with his own checkbook," he wrote.

1920 began with disruption in the Whites' living arrangements. During supper one January evening, shortly before the remodeling of Red Rocks was to begin, a fire broke out on the roof. The family fled. Luckily, only two days earlier Will had purchased another home where the family could live. It was just down the street at 913 Exchange. Now they moved there and the remodeling began.

Red Rocks after remodeling.

Great quantities of the red sandstone from which the original house was built were needed for the remodeling, so Will took it upon himself to find its source. Samples sent to every Chamber of Commerce along the front range of the Rocky Mountains brought a reply from a young man near Colorado Springs. He recognized the sandstone as the kind found in his father's long-closed quarry and offered to reopen it for the Whites at the price of $100 per railroad car. When the work was finished in fall 1921, the front door of Red Rocks faced a different direction and a large porch provided more space for family and friends to gather.

At the 1920 Republican National Convention, Will was a delegate and served on the platform committee. From that convention in Chicago he traveled three weeks later to cover the Democratic convention in San Francisco.

Teenaged Mary, outfitted for a horse-back ride in Colorado.

Much in need of rest, Will retired that summer to the family cabin in Colorado, joined by Sallie, his mother, Sallie's mother, 20-year-old Bill and Mary, who turned

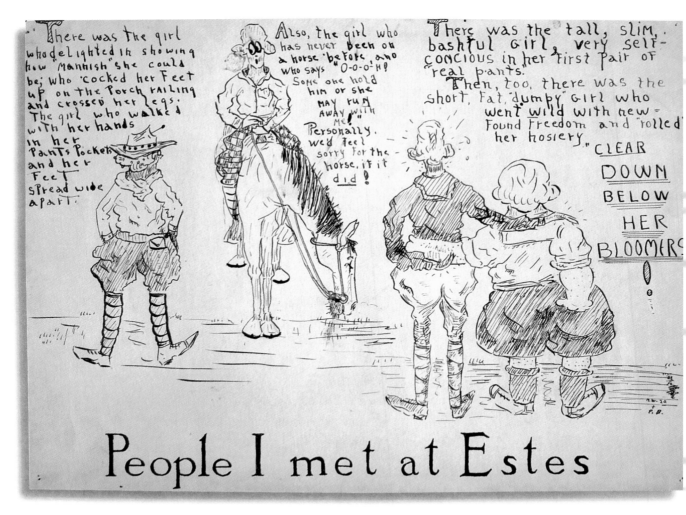

There was the girl who delighted in showing how "Mannish" she could be; who cocked her feet up on the porch railing and crossed her legs. The girl who walked with her hands in her pants pockets and her feet spread wide apart.

Also, the girl who has never been on a horse before and who says "O-o-o-h!" Some one hold him or she may run away with me. Personally, we'd feel sorry for the horse, if it did!

There was the tall, slim, bashful girl, very self-concious in her first pair of real pants.

Then, too, there was the short, fat, dumpy girl who went wild with new-found freedom and rolled her hosiery. "CLEAR DOWN BELOW HER BLOOMERS!"

People I met at Estes

In pictures and words, Mary sketched some of her fellow visitors to the mountains.

16 that June. While Will worked each day in his writing cabin, Bill fished the Big Thompson River for trout, which the family ate for supper. Mary rented out the burros she maintained and spent time at the YMCA grounds. In the evenings there were parties and dances and time for reading by the fire in the cabin.

The Whites entertained many visitors in Colorado, including Jane Addams, and the supper table rarely held only their family. That summer passed in a blur of laughter, music from the phonograph and comings-and-goings from the cabins on the hillside with no hint that it would be the last carefree summer the White family would have.

Facing page: Will on the grounds of his cabin at Moraine Park in Colorado.

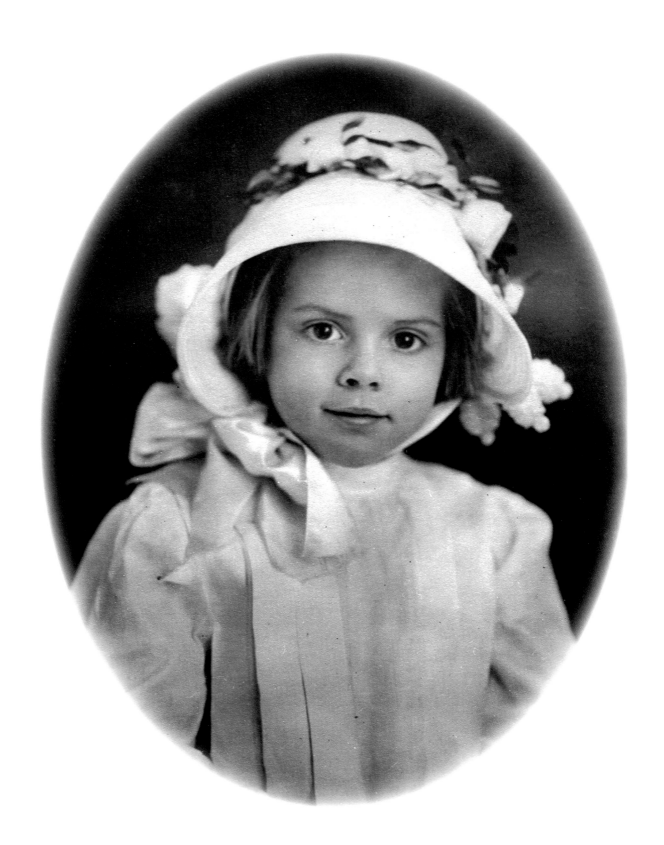

Chapter Nine

Peter Pan

*T*he fall of 1920 found Will involved in supporting the League of Nations, writing editorials against the rise of the Ku Klux Klan in Kansas and traveling to Washington, D.C., to cover the Disarmament Conference for 27 newspapers.

When he traveled to New York to see the movie based on his novel *In the Heart of a Fool*, his daughter, Mary, accompanied him. As he wrote Sallie, the movie was a "mess." Mary asked: "Father, why did you take their money? They haven't used your story."

Bill, who had been attending the University of Kansas, transferred to Harvard that year after convincing his father that he needed the advantages of a prestigious East Coast university. Mary, who was approaching the end of her high school years, applied for entrance to Wellesley, a well-known girls' school also on the East Coast.

Of the Whites' two children, Mary surely commanded the attention of her parents and of townspeople. When she was small, her mother dressed her but as she grew older, her strong sense of self emerged. Mary's clothes reflected her individuality.

Fond of wearing blouses with sailor collars, and on other occasions riding pants and a cowboy hat, she wore her hair in long braids when other girls her age sported upswept styles.

"Mary was full of mischief," a neighbor remembered. "She kept the

65

neighborhood in an uproar but was forgiven because she was generous and could be warmly sympathetic." Her energy, which did not lessen as she grew older, led her into many adventures and sometimes into trouble.

"The whole student body knew about the hours she spent in the outer area of the principal's office awaiting lectures on proper behavior," recalled a friend of her brother's. As a freshman in high school, she once fought a boy almost twice her size, saying, "Well, he'll never pinch me again!"

At school her grades were uneven. When the class was challenging, she met it with success,

Her grades were often good, but Mary couldn't resist letting her mind – and pencil – wander.

but if she was bored or didn't agree with the teacher, her grades reflected it. A look inside her school books shows her energy would not allow her to sit quietly and listen. They are covered with funny sketches and doodles.

As a child she brandished a water pistol at unsuspecting victims, but as a teen she proudly turned to sketching with pen and ink. She was assistant editor of the high school yearbook, *The Re-Echo*, which provided an outlet for her energy and her cartooning during her junior year. That same year, some of her humorous sketches were used in the local college yearbook as well.

Like her father, she loved classical music on the phonograph and reading, but horseback riding was her favorite pastime. Her first ride was a burro, then a Shetland pony, then a mustang and finally saddle horses, which she would guide up the front steps of her grandmother's house next door and into the front

In William Allen White's family, reading was an unending pastime.

room.

She loved matching wits with her father, and he indulged her love of horses.

"She never had but one horse at a time," a local man remembered, "but if her Uncle Charlie knew of a more spirited one, then that's the one she wanted and usually got. Her dad paid for it." Neighborhood children frequently received rides with Mary. She became an excellent rider, but her recklessness worried her mother.

On the afternoon of May 10, 1921, Mary went out on her typical after-school horseback ride through town.

As she rode along Merchant Street, she turned to wave at a high school friend with her bridle hand. The horse veered into a low tree branch in a front yard. Mary's head struck the branch, and she fell to the ground.

At first, the accident appeared to be just another scare. Sallie sent a telegram to Will, who was on the East Coast: "Mary has had another tumble from horse. No scars but severe shock. Horse absolutely has to go. Mary may stand it, but I can't...House moving rapidly...all very grand."

Yet Mary's skull, as it turned out, was fractured. The *Gazette* monitored Mary's condition as she lay in the parlor of the home south of Red Rocks, at one point mentioning that traffic was not allowed on the street in front of the house.

Will went on to Atlantic City, N.J., to speak at the American Booksellers Association convention. Once he arrived there, however, a telegram awaited telling him Mary had taken a turn for the worst. He promptly headed home. When he changed trains at Chicago, two dear friends were waiting to speak to him.

Mary, they said, had died. The date was Friday, May 13.

"It was a long, sad, agonizing journey home," Will reflected. "The Santa Fe stopped the train for me at Exchange Street so that I should not have to go clear to the station, and there Sallie met me. Her face was brave, and her heart was staunch; and when I kissed her I knew it was going to be all right."

Bill made his way from Harvard, but saw the news of his sister's death in newspaper headlines when he changed trains in Kansas City. A childhood friend who picked him up at the station in Emporia remembered him repeating, "Tell me it isn't true." The *Gazette* reported on May 19, 1921, that Mary's grandmother was not told of Mary's death because she had been "...seriously ill for weeks".

All around town, Mary rode her horses. Above right, one of her many braided whips.

Mary's death affected the entire town and, because of her famous father, made headlines around the world through the Associated Press.

The morning after Mary's funeral, Sallie remembered Will saying, "...we must go to the office and take care of Mary." They surprised the *Gazette* staff, entering Will's private office, shutting a door no one recalled ever seeing closed. When they emerged hours later, they had produced what became William Allen White's most widely reprinted piece of writing.

The editorial that Will wrote and that Sallie, as usual, edited brought Mary

MARY WHITE DEAD

Mary Katherine White, only daughter of Mr. and Mrs. W. A. White, died at 5:30 o'clock this morning from an injury received in a fall from a horse Tuesday evening. Her skull was fractured. The exact nature of her injury was not determined until an X-ray picture was taken Wednesday. Yesterday her condition became worse, and Mr. White, who was in the East, and her brother, William, a student at Harvard, were notified. Mr. White will arrive in Emporia tomorrow afternoon and William White is expected tomorrow night or Sunday morning.

The accident which caused her death occurred in a yard on North Merchant Street near the Normal.

The horse she was riding suddenly turned into a driveway, ran into the yard and struck a tree, causing her to fall from the horse.

Mary White was born in Emporia in 1904. She would have been 17 years of age June 18. She attended the city schools and was a junior in the Emporia High School. She is survived by her father and mother and her

to life again for the townspeople to whom she was so familiar. Because it was written for *Gazette* readers, it brimmed with local names and references. When it was reprinted first in the Kansas City *Star* and then eventually around the world, its exceptional detail allowed those who had never met Mary to feel that they knew her and those who knew her but had not attended the funeral feel they had been there. Even those who did not know William Allen White surely felt the strength of his character.

A few weeks later, Will wrote of the editorial: "It has been more widely copied than any other article that has ever appeared in the *Gazette*. From Boston to San Diego, in all the towns, north, south, east, and west, this little article appeared, and I have literally hundreds of letters from men and women who have been touched by it." That same month, Will received a letter from author Christopher Morley requesting permission to include the editorial in a collection of articles. Within a year it appeared in four books used in high school and college reading programs. That trend continued through the years until it had appeared in countless magazines and more than forty anthologies.

Will reflected in his *Autobiography*, "Probably if anything I have written in these long, happy years that I have been earning my living by writing, if anything survives more than a decade beyond my life's span, it will be the thousand words or so that I hammered out on my typewriter that bright May morning under the shadow and agony of Mary's death."

Replying to those many letters of sympathy, beginning to move back into Red Rocks, and finding ways to memorialize Mary helped Will and Sallie fill their suddenly quiet lives. When Mary's high school provided a room for her black schoolmates to relax in, Sallie furnished it and maintained it over the years.

Mary was never far from their minds. On May 10, 1922, they hosted a party at Red Rocks for Mary's graduating high school class. As Will wrote to Bill that day, the event was "...a brilliant affair with more food than would feed a regiment, and a party at the Strand afterward to see Mark Twain's *The Connecticut Yankee*...Mary died a year ago

A note from Sallie to Will, probably the text for a telegram.

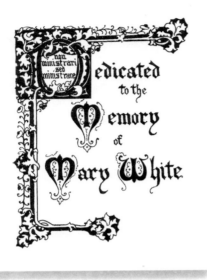

Dedicated to the Memory of Mary White

Saturday. She was hurt a year ago this evening. I am glad Mother is having the party. It helps."

Although Mary never got to attend Wellesley, the girls who would have been her classmates considered her one of them. In their graduating year, 1926, they dedicated the yearbook to her.

That same year, the Whites donated 52 acres of land to the city of Emporia and paid for the landscaping for it to be made into a park in Mary's memory. They stipulated that it should always remain a park and that it should never bear the name of White.

To this day, the park remains, with a name that reflects Mary's sense of adventure and youthful spirit — Peter Pan.

Peter Pan Park in a tinted postcard.

MARY WHITE
The Associated Press reports carrying the news of Mary's White's death declared that it ####### came as the result of a fall from a horse. How she would have hooted at that. She never fell from a horse in her life. Horses have fallen on her and with her-- "I'm always trying to hold 'em in my lap," she used to say. But she was proud of few things, and one was that she could ride anything that had four legs and hair. Her death resulted not from a # fall, but from a blow on the head which fractured her skull and the blow came from the limb of an overhanging tree on the parking.

Will and Sallie's remembrance of Mary White from the Emporia Gazette, May 1921.

Mary White

The Associated Press reports carrying the news of Mary White's death declared that it came as the result of a fall from a horse. How she would have hooted at that! She never fell from a horse in her life. Horses have fallen on her and with her -- "I'm always trying to hold 'em in my lap," she used to say. But she was proud of few things, and one of them was that she could ride anything that had four legs and hair. Her death resulted not from a fall but from a blow on the head which fractured her skull, and the blow came from the limb of an overhanging tree on the parking.

The last hour of her life was typical of its happiness. She came home from a day's work at school, topped off by a hard grind with the copy on the High School Annual, and felt that a ride would refresh her. She climbed into her khakis, chattering to her mother about the work she was doing, and hurried to get her horse and be out on the dirt roads for the country air and the radiant green fields of spring. As she rode through the town on an easy gallop, she kept waving at passers-by. She knew everyone in town. For a decade the little figure in the long pigtail and the red hair ribbon has been familiar on the streets of Emporia, and she got in the way of speaking to those who nodded at her. She passed the Kerrs, walking the horse in front of the Normal Library, and waved at them; passed another friend a few hundred feet farther on, and waved at her.

The horse was walking, and as she turned into North Merchant Street she took off her cowboy hat, and the horse swung into a lope. She passed the Tripletts and waved her cowboy hat at them, still moving gayly north on Merchant Street. A *Gazette* carrier passed -- a High School boy friend -- and she waved at him, but with her bridle hand; the horse veered quickly, plunged into the parking where the low-hanging limb faced her and, while she still looked back waving, the blow came. But she did not fall from the horse; she slipped off, dazed a bit, staggered, and fell in a faint. She never quite recovered consciousness.

But she did not fall from the horse, neither was she riding fast. A year or so ago she used to go like the wind. But that habit was broken, and she used the horse to get into the open, to get fresh, hard exercise, and to work off a certain surplus energy that welled up in her and needed a physical outlet. The need has been in her heart for years. It was back of the impulse that kept the dauntless little brown-clad figure on the streets and country roads of the community and built into a strong, muscular body what had been a frail and sickly frame during the first years of her life. But the riding gave her more than a body. It released a gay and hardy soul. She was the happiest thing in the world. And she was happy because she was enlarging her horizon. She came to know all sorts and conditions of men; Charley O'Brien, the traffic cop, was one of her best friends. W. L. Holtz, the Latin teacher, was another. Tom O'Connor, farmer-politician, and the Rev. J. H. Rice, preacher and police judge, and Frank Beach, music

master, were her special friends; and all the girls, black and white, above the track and below the track, in Pepville and Stringtown, were among her acquaintances. And she brought home riotous stories of her adventures. She loved to rollick; persiflage was her natural expression at home. Her humor was a continual bubble of joy. She seemed to think in hyperbole and metaphor. She was mischievous without malice, as full of faults as an old shoe. No angel was Mary White, but an easy girl to live with for she never nursed a grouch five minutes in her life.

With all her eagerness for the out-of-doors, she loved books. On her table when she left her room were a book by Conrad, one by Galsworthy, "Creative Chemistry" by E. E. Slosson, and a Kipling book. She read Mark Twain, Dickens, and Kipling before she was ten -- all of their writings. Wells and Arnold Bennett particularly amused and diverted her. She was entered as a student in Wellesley for 1922; was assistant editor of the High School Annual this year, and in line for election to the editorship next year. She was a member of the executive committee of the High School Y.W.C.A.

Within the last two years she had begun to be moved by an ambition to draw. She began as most children do by scribbling in her school books, funny pictures. She bought cartoon magazines and took a course -- rather casually, naturally, for she was, after all, a child with no strong purposes -- and this year she tasted the first fruits of success by having her pictures accepted by the High School Annual. But the thrill of delight she got when Mr. Ecord, of the Normal Annual, asked her to do the cartooning for that book this spring, was too beautiful for words. She fell to her work with all her enthusiastic heart. Her drawings were accepted, and her pride -- always repressed by a lively sense of the ridiculous figure she was cutting -- was a really gorgeous thing to see. No successful artist every drank a deeper draft of satisfaction than she took from the little fame her work was getting among her schoolfellows. In her glory, she almost forgot her horse -- but never her car.

Mary's own calendar, marked off to the day she went on her last ride.

For she used the car as a jitney bus. It was her social life. She never had a "party" in all her nearly seventeen years -- wouldn't have one; but she never drove a block in her life that she didn't begin to fill the car with pick-ups! Everybody rode with Mary White--white and black, old and young, rich and poor, men and women. She like nothing better than to fill the car with long-legged High School boys and an occasional girl, and parade the town. She never had a "date," nor went to a dance, except once with her brother Bill, and the "boy proposition" didn't interest her -- yet. But young people -- great spring-breaking, varnish-cracking, fender-bending, door-sagging carloads of "kids"-- gave her great pleasure. Her zests were keen. But the most fun she ever had in her life was acting as chairman of the committee that got up the big turkey dinner for the poor folks at the county home; scores of pies, gallons of slaw, jam, cakes, preserves, oranges, and a wilderness of turkey were loaded into the car and taken to the county home. And, being of a practical turn of mind, she risked her own Christmas dinner to see that the poor folks actually got it all. Not that she was a cynic; she just disliked to tempt folks. While there, she found a blind colored uncle, very old, who could do nothing but make rag rugs, and she rustled up from her school friends rags enough to keep him busy for a season. The last engagement she tried to make was to take the guests at the county home out for a car ride. And the last endeavor of her life was to try to get a rest room for colored girls in the High School. She found one girl reading in the toilet, because there was no better place for a colored girl to loaf, and it inflamed her sense of injustice and she became a nagging harpy to those who she thought could remedy the evil. The poor she always had with her and was glad of it. She hungered and thirsted for righteousness; and was the most impious creature in the world. She joined the church without consulting her parents, not particularly for her soul's good. She never had a thrill of piety in her life, and would have hooted at a "testimony." But even as a little child, she felt the church was an agency for helping people to more of life's abundance, and she wanted to help. She never wanted help for herself. Clothes meant little to her. It was a fight to get a new rig on her; but eventually a harder fight to get it off. She never wore a jewel and had no ring but her High School class ring and never asked for anything but a wrist watch. She refused to have her hair up, though she was nearly seventeen. "Mother," she protested," you don't know how much I get by with, in my braided pigtails, that I could not with my hair up." Above every other passion of her life was her passion not to grow up, to be a child. The tomboy in her, which was big, seemed loath to be put away forever in skirts. She was a Peter Pan who refused to grow up.

Her funeral yesterday at the Congregational Church was as she would have wished it; no singing, no flowers except the big bunch of red roses from her brother Bill's Harvard classmen -- heavens, how proud that would have made her! -- and the red roses from the *Gazette* forces, in vases, at her head and feet. A short prayer: Paul's beautiful essay on "Love" from the Thirteenth Chapter of First Corinthians; some remarks about her democratic spirit by her friend, John H. J. Rice, pastor and police judge, which she would have deprecated if she could; a prayer sent down for her by her friend Carl Nau; and, opening the service, the slow, poignant movement from Beethoven's Moonlight Sonata, which she loved; and closing the service a cutting from the joyously melancholy first movement of Tchaikovsky's Pathetic Symphony, which she liked to hear, in certain moods, on the phonograph, then the Lord's Prayer by her friends in High School.

MARY WHITE
BORN JUNE 18, 1904
DIED MAY 13, 1921

That was all.

For her pallbearers only her friends were chosen: her Latin teacher, W. L. Holtz; her High School principal, Rice Brown; her doctor, Frank Foncannon; her friend, W. W. Finney; her pal at the *Gazette* office, Walter Hughes; and her brother Bill. It would have made her smile to know that her friend, Charley O'Brien, the traffic cop had been transferred from Sixth and Commercial to the corner near the church to direct her friends who came to bid her good-by.

A rift in the clouds in a gray day threw a shaft of sunlight upon her coffin as her nervous, energetic little body sank to its last sleep. But the soul of her, the glowing, gorgeous, fervent soul of her, surely was flaming in eager joy upon some other dawn.

Keeping Up the Game

*I*n the months after Mary's death the Whites worked to maintain an upbeat outlook, but the loss forever changed their lives, and it took them time to adjust to it. They moved back into their remodeled home in summer 1921. The upstairs room that Mary had designed for herself was used as a sewing room for Sallie. Its sunny orientation made it a soothing retreat.

The editorial about Mary's death had the same public impact as "What's the Matter with Kansas?" and job offers came Will's way. He accepted a few opportunities to write weekly articles for New York magazines and newspapers but flatly refused to leave Emporia. A bright spot in 1921 was the opening of a motion picture based on Will's first novel, *A Certain Rich Man*.

Before Mary died, Will had started a biography of his good friend Theodore Roosevelt. After her death he was unable to return to it. In his mind it remained tied to his daughter.

Sallie White found solace in books.

The cabin at Estes Park sat empty. A summer there without its liveliest inhabitant would have been too much to bear. As Will wrote to a well-wisher: "Mrs. White and I are standing on our feet, realizing that the loss is heavy and the blow is hard, but not beating our hands against the bars and asking why. On our books Mary is a net gain. She was worth so much more than she cost, and she left so much more behind than she took away that we are flooded with joyous memories and cannot question either the goodness of God or the general decency of man."

Privately, to his son, Will acknowledged that he was "keeping up the game" of going to work each day. Sallie, he said, was still "wracked with grief....I think when Mother gets better I will be stronger."

A railroad strike in summer 1922 brought Will one of the greatest challenges of his career. Emporia had a large number of railroad workers, and young Bill, on his summer vacation from Harvard, covered the strikers' meetings for the *Gazette*.

Across Kansas, merchants who supported the strikers placed large signs in their windows stating, "We are for the strikers 100 percent." The governor of Kansas, Henry J. Allen, issued an order that the signs be removed. Until that time, there had been no sign in the *Gazette*'s window, but when Will heard about the order, he defiantly put up his own sign.

"Instead of 100 percent, we have started it at 49 percent," he told *Gazette* readers. "If the strike lasts until tomorrow, we shall change the per cent to 50, and move it up a little every day."

The governor and Will had been friends for years, but Will did not agree with this limit on freedom of speech. Will wanted to see how far his friend — and the Kansas judicial system — were willing to go. As he expected, a warrant was issued for his arrest on July 22. He made sure the event occurred so it would be featured in the Sunday newspapers, which were read by more people than the daily papers.

The story of Will's impending arrest was indeed covered by Kansas newspapers and then spread across the nation. However, the matter was arranged so that Will's lawyer accepted the charges and posted bond for him. Will never spent a day in jail. The sign, meanwhile, came down.

Three days afterward, Governor Allen spoke at the Emporia State Teacher's

College and was introduced by Will. The event made national headlines.

As the legal question simmered, Will replied on July 27 to a letter from a friend who disagreed with what he had done. He was so pleased with the reply that he used it as his editorial that day under the title "To an Anxious Friend."

In defense of freedom of speech, he wrote, "The orderly business of life will go forward if only men can speak in whatever way given them to utter whatever their hearts hold." The editorial struck a chord with people, and again something Will wrote to alleviate his own concerns spread across the nation through its newspapers. Although the case against Will was eventually dropped, he was awarded the Pulitzer Prize for editorial writing the next May.

Mary Ann Hatten White in her later years.

His friendship with Henry Allen never wavered.

"The deepest friendship makes the firmest and fondest faith, not the closest agreement," he later wrote to Mrs. Allen.

Another loss struck the White family in May 1924. Mary Ann Hatten White — who stood up to the townspeople of Council Grove as a young school teacher, who raised her son after the death of his father, and who supported her son as he rose to worldwide fame — died at nearly 95 years of age. In an editorial written the day after his mother's death, Will observed, "For nearly thirty years she had lived in this town, most of the time in her own house, and always in her own way."

Allen White's grave, along with that of baby Frederick, had been moved from El Dorado to Emporia after the death of Mary White. Mary Ann Hatten White's name now joined her husband's and infant son's on the cemetery marker.

Chapter Eleven

Laughing 'em Out of Kansas

*T*he Whites joined friends in 1923 on a cruise of the Mediterranean, and found a new battle awaiting them on their return to Emporia.

The Ku Klux Klan had firmly established itself in Emporia and was looking to expand its influence in the 1924 election for governor. By the 1920s the Klan had widened its scope, targeting Jews, Catholics and immigrants along with the black people that the organization had always threatened. Will had been one of the few newspaper editors in Kansas to take note of the Klan's presence in the early 1920s. He had not minced words.

"It is an organization of cowards," he wrote in the *Gazette* August 2, 1921. "Not a man in it has the courage of his convictions."

*Facing page: Discarding briefly his pledge never to run for office,
Will campaigned for governor of Kansas in 1924.*

Will, Sallie and friends in Egypt, part of their 1923 journey around the Mediterranean.

Will wrote young Bill at Harvard in 1922, "The K.K.K. people seem to be having a grand old time and we are having lots of fun fighting them."

Over the years, Will not only attacked the group editorially but also exposed its members. Secrecy is at the heart of the hood-wearing Klan, but the *Gazette* regularly published lists of those attending the meetings, labeling them "kluxers".

Once, a Klan state meeting was held at the new Broadview Hotel in Emporia. Reporter and later managing editor Frank Clough remembered how Will requested — and got — the hotel register. From it, names of attendees were printed in the *Gazette*. In the same issue, White's editorial otherwise praised the new hotel. He told Clough: "Always remember after you spank a child, you should give it a piece of candy. It makes everyone feel better."

80

White Announces

I have filed my petition for governor and am in this race to win. It is the largest independent petition ever filed for an office in Kansas. Over three times more names were signed to these petitions for Carr Taylor and myself for lieutenant governor and governor than were needed. None of these petitions came from my home town or county. I wished honestly to test sentiment. There can be no doubt about the sentiment. The issue in Kansas this year is the Ku Klux Klan above everything. The Ku Klux Klan is found in nearly every county. It represents a small minority of the citizenship and it is organized for purposes of terror. Its terror is directed at honest, law-abiding citizens, Negroes, Jews and Catholics. These groups in Kansas comprise more than one-fourth of our population. They are entitled to their full constitutional rights; their rights to life, liberty and the pursuit of happiness. They

the one phrase that all klan use when denying their mem ship.

The Democratic guberna nominee, Jonathan M. Davis er, before the primary or has uttered one syllable would offend the most a klansman. He had the kla dorsement in the primary. party threw it over, but Dav not disclaimed it.

So here are the two·majo ties in Kansas led in the rac governor by men who had support in the primary and will not disavow that suppo day. A man who has not the age nor does not rise in eous indignation to denounc defy the Ku Klux Klan in th mary and in the election, going.to oppose it seriously, governor's office.

I want to be governor t Kansas from the disgrace o Ku Klux Klan. And I wa

By fall 1924, with the election for governor looming, both major-party candidates for governor were tainted by association with the Klan. Will urged politically active friends to run for governor as independents, but none of them would agree. With the election only six weeks away, Will — the editor who vowed he would never seek political office — made a surprising announcement.

"I have filed my petition for governor and am in this race to win," he wrote in the *Gazette* September 20, 1924. "I want to be governor to free Kansas from the disgrace of the Ku Klux Klan. And I want to offer Kansans afraid of the Klan and ashamed of that disgrace a candidate who shares their fear and shame."

The candidate and his campaign car journeyed from Emporia to all parts of Kansas.

Using his own money, Will set out on a campaign tour. He said his aim was to "laugh the Klan out of Kansas." With son Bill driving the old family car and Sallie along to help, the Whites traveled 2,783 miles across the state. Will made 104 speeches, spreading the word of his candidacy and the reason for it. The national media followed him, some of them supportive, others painting him as foolish. A reporter even came from the London *Daily News* to cover the campaign for its readers. New York *Times* correspondent Anne O'Hare McCormick remembered Will as "a stout little Don Quixote riding a Ford and chuckling as he went."

The Whites returned to Red Rocks the night before the election, tired but exhilarated. Will spent election day working at the *Gazette*. He fended off reporters who wanted to cover his election-night activities.

"You can't watch me, because I'm going to bed," he told a reporter for the Kansas City *Star*. "I have made my fight for what I believe and I'm tired and going to sleep in my own bed for the first time in weeks."

Although his campaign speeches had rung with hope for his chances, on the morning after the election Will was not surprised to find that the Republican candidate, Ben Paulen, had won and that he had come in last. Yet Will's anti-Klan campaign had gained more than 149,000 votes. In addition he was pleased to see that three anti-Klan candidates for other state offices on the Republican ticket had won. He had encouraged their candidacies along with his own, and their elections ensured that there would be plenty of opposition to the Klan among statewide officials.

With Will's colorful words echoing in their ears, Kansas people did laugh the Klan out of the state by 1926. In an editorial that year, Will chuckled: "The kluxers in Kansas are as dejected and sad as a last year's bird nest..."

"A real American goes hunting." An editorial cartoon from The New York World.

Besides running for governor in 1924, Will completed a biography of former President Woodrow Wilson, a book that he had been working on for five years. Also that year, he supported Calvin Coolidge's campaign for president. His research on Coolidge for a magazine article led to a hastily written biography published in 1925.

Now in his late 50s, Will was known around the world as someone who could be counted on to give a thoughtful opinion on national or world affairs. He visited Hawaii with a group of American delegates to a conference on Pacific countries and sent back to the *Gazette* reports on the session and on the islands themselves.

A meeting of Book-of-the-Month Club judges.

Wearing the top hats and long coats of diplomats, Will, left, stood with a presidential delegation to Haiti.

In 1926 he was asked to join three other well-known literary people as a judge for the new Book-of-the-Month Club, an organization that each month shipped books recommended by the judges to subscribers across the United States. Will took the idea seriously, looking over 20 or so books sent to him each month by publishers and giving his opinions either at meetings in New York City or by telegram. It was a position he held the rest of his life.

The next time a presidential election came around, Will was 60 and ready to plunge in wholeheartedly for the Republication candidate. In 1928 that candidate was Herbert Hoover. Will spoke on his behalf in Kansas, Georgia, North Carolina and Tennessee, and when Hoover won, Will's political involvement increased. Will's old friend Henry J. Allen also was appointed to the U.S. Senate. Will began to ride the train between Emporia and Washington almost as much as when Theodore Roosevelt had been in office.

Nearing his 62nd birthday, Will received word that President Hoover had appointed him to a commission to review conditions on the island of Haiti. When he returned, the stock market crash of 1929 plunged the U.S. into a major depression, but *Gazette* editorials continued to support the leadership of Hoover. In turn, Hoover appointed Will to the President's Committee for Unemployment Relief, a cause Will also headed in his hometown.

As before, when he was involved in too many things at once, Will suffered from nervous exhaustion and had to spend six months recuperating in California and Colorado. He returned ready to serve as an interpreter of events as the United States headed toward another world war.

Chapter Twelve

The Sage of Emporia

*T*oward the end of President Herbert Hoover's term in office in 1932, millions of people were out of work and homeless because of the Great Depression. Even a firm Republican like Will had to acknowledge that the country wanted action. Despite the fact that Franklin Delano Roosevelt was a Democrat, Will liked his idea of a "New Deal" to give a new chance to Americans down on their luck.

Will covered the 1932 Democratic and Republican national conventions, and as a staunch Republican campaigned again for Hoover and also for his friend Alf Landon, who was running for governor of Kansas. He wrote editorials favoring all the Republican candidates and gave a speech that was broadcast nationwide. Yet people were ready for new leadership, and the confidence of Roosevelt encouraged them. Roosevelt defeated Hoover in a landslide. Despite Democratic victories in many races, Alf Landon was elected governor of Kansas.

Once Roosevelt became president, he appointed an old friend of Will's, Harold Ickes, as secretary of the interior. With Landon as governor, Will's political involvement in the state and national capitals was ensured for several more years.

The presidency of this Roosevelt would span the rest of Will's life. Although he disagreed politically many times with the Democratic president, Will grew to respect Roosevelt's popularity and his command of foreign policy. It was said of Will that he was on Roosevelt's side three and one-half out of every four years —

It was said that Will, an ardent Republican, was on President Franklin D. Roosevelt's side 3 1/2 of every four years ~ except, that is, at election time. In autographing this photo, the president quipped that he was on White's side "all 48 months."

except during election campaigns. Roosevelt became one of many important people Will could disagree with yet remain a friend.

After Roosevelt's inauguration in 1933, Will and Sallie embarked on another tour of Europe, starting in London where Will reported on the International Economic Conference. The North American Newspaper Alliance distributed his articles in the United States. The Whites also visited Italy, Austria and Russia. On his return to America, Will voiced concern about conditions in Europe as Adolf Hitler began his rise to power.

Turning sixty-five in 1933 caused Will to reflect: "I have never had a bored hour in my life. I get up every morning now wondering what new strange, gorgeous thing is going to happen and it always happens at fairly reasonable intervals....Lady Luck has been good to me."

Advancing age did not keep Will from involvement in politics, nor did it keep him from expressing his opinion. He continued to write for national magazines, gave speeches across the country and worked on a second biography of Calvin Coolidge. His wisdom on issues of the day was respected across the United States, earning him the nickname "The Sage of Emporia." People who had read his articles and editorials wrote to him and were sure to receive a personal reply. Will loved to write letters and kept carbon copies of them all.

When Walter Hughes, the long-time Gazette manager, died in 1932, Bill took over as business manager. One of Bill's first achievements was remodeling the second floor of the *Gazette* building into offices, which were rented out to doctors and dentists. In 1934 Bill left the "Emporia *Gazette* School of Journalism" for the East Coast, taking

A letter to the president of a local college demonstrated Will's techniques of persuasion.

THE EMPORIA GAZETTE
W. A. WHITE, EDITOR AND OWNER
W. L. WHITE, PUBLISHER
EMPORIA, KANSAS

March 1,1

Dear Tom:

We have not made a call for the dues for the Pet
Pan Pageant Association for a year and a half. We have
on our surplus, somewhat by cutting down expenses, but we
are now clear flat busted, and we shall have to ask the m
bers to renew their subscriptions.

We are hoping that we can get Mr. Gilson to put
"Twelfth Night" this summer, and if he does, it ought to
most beautiful. I still think Shakespeare is better than
modern plays.

I am asking Mr. Robinson to tell me what you gav
the last time and will attach the amount with a clip to
letter, and I hope you can duplicate your subscription.

Mrs. White and I are doing well out here. I hav
been exceptionally well and she is slowly gaining streng
I hope to see you soon.

With warm personal regards, I am

Sincerely yours,

Mr. Thos. W. Butcher,
Emporia, Kansas.

with him his wife, the former Kathrine Klinkenberg, whom he'd married in 1931 while she was on the staff of *Time* magazine. After Bill worked on the staff of a Washington, D.C., newspaper, they settled in New York, where both worked on newspapers and magazines.

In November 1935 Will and Sallie embarked on a tour of Asia, starting with the Philippines. There they attended the inauguration of the islands' president. They found the Far East fascinating and collected items for their home. When they returned, Will dived into the 1936 presidential campaign, observing the action on both sides. This time his Kansas friend Alf Landon was running for president and Will did what he could to help, but the Roosevelt tide was too strong, even in Kansas. Roosevelt's victory over Landon in November 1936 came as no surprise.

Public sentiment toward Will reached new heights in 1938 when he turned 70. Arriving at the *Gazette* office on his birthday that year, he was greeted by hundreds of Emporia residents and a brass band. More than a hundred people sent him flowers, and birthday cards and telegrams flooded the office from all over the United States. Newspapers and magazines across the country mentioned his

THE EMPORIA GAZETTE

W. A. White..................................Editor
W. L. White..................................Publisher

PUBLISHED DAILY EXCEPT SUNDAY
Official Paper of Lyon County
and city of Emporia, Kansas

Telephones..................................48 and 49

To the end of Will's and Sallie's lives, Red Rocks remained their Emporia haven.

birthday and his contribution to American life.

In an editorial published on February 5, 1938, and widely circulated, Will shared his personal philosophy: "I am not afraid of tomorrow for I have seen yesterday and I love today." Both *Life* and *Look* magazines featured articles on him, and he spoke by invitation to organizations across the nation. He gave a series of lectures at Harvard University that were published the next year in a book entitled *The Changing West*. The American Society of Newspaper Editors elected him their president, and his second Coolidge biography was published.

Boys' and Girls' Wantads For A Nickel in The Gazette

In The Gazette tomorrow will appear the announcement of a special want ad section for boys and girls. Beginning Saturday boys and girls of 16 years and under may run their own want ads in this special section to buy, sell, or trade children's articles or advertise for jobs.

All want ads must be brought or mailed to The Gazette accompanied by 5 cents and the articles must be things that boys and girls want.

Each ad must contain the name, address and age of the child and contain not more than 25 words.

Hundreds of boys and girls read The Gazette every day, and this is their opportunity to make some spare money before school opens by placing ads in their own want ad section. Of course, advertising on this offer will be subject to approval and The Gazette ad department reserves the right to rewrite or reject any copy. Watch tomorrow's paper for complete rules.

Former *Gazette* employee Oscar Stauffer commented in the Arkansas City *Daily Traveler*, "Many persons living in Kansas fail to appreciate how William Allen White towers in the world."

He would need this stature to endure the pace of the coming years.

Facing page: Will at his desk at the Gazette.

Chapter Thirteen

A National Institution

$\mathcal{A}$s an observer of world affairs, Will had long been concerned about the trouble brewing in Europe, trouble he had observed firsthand in 1933 .

When the second world war broke out in September 1939, he was quick to support President Roosevelt in calling for repeal of the Neutrality Law, which prohibited the sale of arms and ammunition to nations at war. With the law out of the way, countries battling Hitler could acquire weapons from the United States. A nationwide committee was formed to encourage public support, and Will was asked to head it.

Although the secretary of state himself had recommended Will for the position, at the age of 71 Will was reluctant to accept. He had planned to spend his remaining years in Emporia, working on his autobiography. The committee job would require trips to Washington and New York, and close contact with the president and his advisors. Yet it also would help him pursue two wishes he had expressed in editorials: keep the United States out of the war in Europe and contribute to the fall of Hitler.

With the encouragement of friends in New York and Washington he agreed,

Facing page: Will grew accustomed to broadcasting over network radio.

and the Non-Partisan Committee for Peace through Revision of the Neutrality Law began its work with Will at its head. He addressed the nation by radio on October 15, 1939, and visited with members of Congress about the situation. In early November the bill to repeal the law passed.

"This was the first time I ever had hold of a lever that controlled a national current," Will told his readers on November 6, 1939. "It was interesting — but scary!"

As the Whites watched events unfold from afar, their son Bill went to Europe to cover the war for more than 50 newspapers and CBS radio. His byline was William Lindsay White. Pride filled Will and Sallie as they read Bill's stories in newspapers and listened to his voice on the radio. When a newsreel from the war zone in Finland with brief shots of Bill showed for four days in an Emporia theatre, the Whites watched it seven times!

William Lindsay White broadcasting from Finland as the war raged in Europe.

Bill's overseas journey also brought Will and Sallie a grandchild. Bill and Kathrine adopted an English war orphan named Barbara. His war experiences also provided Bill material for several books that were made into movies, including an account of Barbara's adoption, *Journey for Margaret*.

Early in 1940, Will helped First Lady Eleanor Roosevelt and his friend Dorothy Canfield Fisher launch the Children's Crusade, through which American schoolchildren collected money to assist needy children in Europe. By May of that year, the need for another organization to assist the Allies

Barbara White, a war orphan adopted by William L. and Kathrine White and subject of a book and movie.

fighting in Europe became clear. Again, Will was asked to head the group, called the Committee to Defend America by Aiding the Allies.

From his study in Red Rocks, Will watched the committee grow to 300 branches all over the country. In June, Will and the committee published a book of articles entitled *Defense for America* explaining the need for U.S. assistance to the countries fighting Hitler. Will wrote the introduction, and free copies were sent to teachers, governors, ministers and businessmen. In the midst of this work, Will covered the national presidential conventions and supported the presidential campaign of Republican Wendell Willkie.

In editorials, he urged Roosevelt not to seek a third term but to serve as an advisor to a new president. Nevertheless, Roosevelt ran and was re-elected in November 1940. By then, there were 750 chapters of the "White Committee," as it had come to be called. Will urged members to "take off our political buttons and wear just one button 'Defend America by Aiding the Allies'." Although the committee enjoyed widespread support, Will received angry letters and read newspaper editorials accusing him of leading America into the war. He denied that in a widely reprinted letter to a friend, saying, "The only reason in God's world I am in this organization is to keep this country out of war."

World affairs did not keep Will from trying to head off a problem in his home state. Artist John Steuart Curry was painting John Brown in a mural on the Kansas Capitol's second floor. When the work met with criticism, Will sent strong words his way in a letter: "...whatever you do, don't take the John Brown away from Kansas. It is destined

Too fiery for some Kansans, this was abolitionist John Brown as depicted in the Kansas Capitol by John Steuart Curry.

to be one of the greatest pictures of our country. It has for me all the appeal of Michelangelo's 'Moses'. It seems to me that it is your greatest work to date." The striking portrait now known around the world remained in the mural, becoming, as Will predicted in an earlier letter, "...a place of pilgrimage."

The fierce pace and public scrutiny began to take its toll on 72-year-old Will's health and at one point his doctor insisted he stay in bed for two weeks. Even then, phone calls and telegrams kept coming. By the end of December 1940, with Sallie also having fallen ill, he resigned as chairman of the "White Committee" to take effect January 1, 1941.

"The job was too big a one for me," he told *Gazette* readers, "and after all, I have my own life to live, and again after all I wanted to celebrate my 73rd birthday in peace and devote the year or two or three that may be left to me to writing some books and helping with some chores around the house here in Emporia and Kansas."

The New York *Times* commented on his contribution to the committee in an editorial on January 4, 1941, "His name and personality made the White Committee a going concern in its first and difficult days...We do know that this would be a poorer, more cynical, less generous country without Will White of Emporia."

Will and Sallie retreated to the warm weather of Arizona. When Sallie's health did not improve they visited the Mayo Clinic in Minnesota and were both told to slow down. That spring, Will drastically reduced the hours he spent at the *Gazette*, although he still wrote editorials when he had something to say. Many of his editorials reflected his fear that the United States would have to enter the war, and that the country would be attacked. That was exactly what happened. Japanese bombers attacked Pearl Harbor in the Hawaiian Islands, then a U.S. territory, on December 7, 1941.

Will and Sallie and another good-humored character.

By that time, Will was back to working longer days at the *Gazette* because of a staff shortage. Before he left for the office each morning, Will spent time writing the autobiography he was determined to finish before he died. He kept a strict schedule, arriving at the *Gazette* at 9 a.m. to answer letters and oversee newspaper matters, going home for lunch and a short

Sallie, Bill and Will together again on the porch at Red Rocks.

nap, and returning to work on his editorials until 5:30 p.m. The days of a brisk walk to work and hours spent at the typewriter were over. Sallie or the White's cook drove him each day, and all his writing was dictated to a secretary who typed it.

With a war on, it seemed impossible for Will to stick only to his book and to the *Gazette*. He became state chairman of the War Bond drive and one of the national directors of the Red Cross. In 1942, he took on his last political campaign, supporting Andrew Schoeppel for governor of Kansas. When Schoeppel won, Will went back to commenting on the political scene, observing in early 1943 that President Roosevelt possessed a "constructive imagination."

Will's 75th birthday in 1943 again brought a flood of appreciation to his

Sallie and Will at the window seat of their cabin in the Rockies in 1943. At the foot of the mountain in the distance was the cabin where they had honeymooned half a century before.

door. *Time* magazine simply stated, "Americans wished the U.S. had more editors like him" and the local Rotary Club gave him 75 red roses.

Later that year, when they were in New York for a Book-of-the-Month Club meeting, both Will and Sallie became ill.

"We go hand in hand, Mr. White and I, even in influenza," Sallie told reporters. They had planned to repeat their honeymoon trip of 50 years earlier but canceled it when Will developed pneumonia. By June, they were able to travel to their beloved cabin near Estes Park, Colorado. Will enjoyed hours simply sitting on the porch observing Longs Peak. It would be his last visit to the cabin.

In October 1943 Will submitted what would be his last articles for the North American Newspaper Alliance. Later that month, after an operation at the Mayo Clinic, cancer was discovered in his digestive tract. While news of the diagnosis appeared in a small note on the second page of the *Gazette*, other newspapers featured it on their front pages. More cards, letters and telegrams arrived at the clinic in Minnesota and at Red Rocks in Emporia. Will knew he would be unable to finish his autobiography, so he entrusted its conclusion to Bill. With the help of a nurse, Sallie cared for him at home.

In a letter to a long-time friend, she described Will's decline: "Each day shows a loss of strength. He doesn't read any more, not even the headlines in the papers....There are flashes of the old Will, just glimmers, not flashes, and I haven't seen him smile for weeks. There is just nothing that can be done."

As Will's condition worsened, and his visits to the *Gazette* became impossible, Bill moved to Emporia with his family and began to assume his father's job. Near the end, Will had one request: "Ask the boys to come to the house" and *Gazette* employees climbed the steps of Red Rocks to say goodbye to their dying employer.

On the occasion of Will's 75th birthday in 1943, Oscar Stauffer had commented in the Topeka *State Journal*, "...Kansas is William Allen White and William Allen White is Kansas..." On the

A GREAT INTERPRETER LEAVES THE SCENE.

WILLIAM ALLEN WHITE
1868–1944

A farewell from the Kansas City Star.

morning of the birthday of Kansas, January 29, 1944, William Allen White died at his home on Exchange Street.

Tributes poured in. One came in a telegram from President Roosevelt: "The newspaper world loses one of its wisest and most beloved editors in the death of William Allen White. He made the Emporia *Gazette* a national institution...To me his passing brings a real sense of personal loss for we had been the best of friends for years."

Newspapers around the world carried obituaries and front-page headlines announcing his death. The people of Emporia "...began to realize that their neighbor of fifty years was a man who somehow had gained international stature."

Will's body lay in state on a lounge chair in his study at Red Rocks, and word passed

that Sallie invited all his friends to come and bid farewell. In the days before his funeral, a steady stream of people of all colors and stations of life flowed through Red Rocks. On January 31, the *Gazette* employees, the governor of Kansas and many out-of-town friends joined hundreds of locals in the funeral procession from Red Rocks to the College of Emporia

An Era in American Journalism Ends With W. A. White's Death

There Has Been None Like the Kansas Editor, in Literature and Civic Leadership, in This Democracy in Its 160 Years.

By Paul I. Wellman.

WILLIAM ALLEN WHITE was born February 10, 1868, at Emporia, the son of Dr. and Mrs. Allen White. When he was 2 years old his family moved to El Dorado, Kas., where Dr. White became at once a leader in the struggles of that pioneer community. The Emporia edi- use his own words, "I wrote three letters to El Dorado, my home town. One to George Tolle, who ran a grocery store there; one to Cass Friedlburg, who ran a dry goods store, and one to T. P. Fulton, asking each of them for a job. George Tolle and Cass Friedlburg knew my desultory ways and rejected my job suggestion. T. P. Fulton (who pub-

chapel. Pallbearers were six *Gazette* staffers longest employed at the newspaper.

Will's funeral resembled that of his daughter, Mary, which he had planned. There were Tschaikovsky's *Symphonie Pathetique*, the 23rd Psalm read and a reading from the 13th Chapter of First Corinthians. Mrs. White had given the minister a copy of the sermon from Mary's funeral, saying that almost everything said of the daughter could be said of her father. Henry Haskell, editor of the Kansas City *Star*, spoke on Will's life and work, saying, "He was a great interpreter of the human spectacle, be it comedy or tragedy."

An attendee later observed: "If he could have arranged to attend his own funeral, Mr. White would have been pleased. The church was 'packed to the rafters' and loud speakers blared the sermon and the music to the throng outside. 'Everyone' was there—the common man as well as the 'high and mighty'."

An estimated 1,800 people attended the brief service at Maplewood Cemetery in Emporia, where Will was buried near Mary.

"In the cemetery, in the dying sun, under the dead trees," a Chicago *Sun* reporter wrote, "William Allen White was only a tired editor gone home to greet his little girl."

Chapter Fourteen

Lasting Legacy

*I*t didn't take long for Will's friends in Kansas and on both coasts to find ways to honor his memory and ensure that future generations knew the name of William Allen White.

A memorial foundation was established in Emporia shortly after his death and within a month a memorial booklet was issued by the Book-of-the-Month Club in New York City. Before he died Will learned he was to receive the first gold medal for distinguished service from the American Society of Newspaper Editors. It was awarded in April 1944, three months after his death.

In May 1944 the S.S. William Allen White, a cargo ship that carried materials for the war effort, was launched at a shipyard in Richmond, California. A war bond drive in Emporia financed a B-29 bomber for the war effort, and named it the *William Allen White*.

When Will attended the University of Kansas in the 1880s, there was no school of journalism, but within a year of his death the Kansas Board of Regents established the William Allen White School of Journalism and Public Information. Friends both professional and personal chartered the William

Allen White Foundation in 1944, which became affiliated with the school of journalism to "emphasize and broaden an understanding of journalism, to which Mr. White devoted his life."

True to his word, Will's son finished the autobiography and in 1947 it won the Pulitzer Prize in letters. The U.S. Post Office department issued a 3-cent stamp honoring Will in 1948.

The B-29 William Allen White

The first public memorial to Will in Emporia was dedicated in 1950. A likeness of him sculpted by artist Jo Davidson overlooks the pond in Peter Pan Park with the Mary White editorial engraved on its base. Former president Herbert Hoover spoke at its dedication.

Sallie White played a major role in preserving Will's letters and manuscripts, donating them to the Library of Congress, to what is now Emporia State University and to the University of Kansas. She lived on at Red Rocks, dying in her sleep in the hospital six years after her husband, on December 29, 1950. She was 81. A few days later, Whitley Austin of the *Salina Journal*, a former *Gazette* employee, recognized her important role: "Behind nearly every man whose fame rests on kindness and understanding as well as ambition, may be found the influence of a good woman. Such a woman was Sallie White....Whatever Mr. White did or wrote or said, if it was worth doing, writing, or saying, reflected her wise, kindly influence...."

In the last year of Sallie's life, an elementary school dedicated to Will's memory was built across the street from Red Rocks. Sallie could watch its construction from the east windows of Red Rocks and took a tour in her

Former President Herbert Hoover, left, with William Lindsay White at the dedication of a bust in Peter Pan Park.

The William Allen White School of Journalism at the University of Kansas in the late 1960s.

wheelchair before it opened in November 1950. William Allen White elementaries can also be found in Wichita and Kansas City.

In 1952, Emporia State University's new library, the William Allen White Library, was dedicated. In its basement is the Mary White Room, which houses a collection of children's books as well as some of Mary's belongings and other items on loan from the White family. American novelist Upton Sinclair commented in a letter of appreciation for the library's grand opening brochure: "It was a lovely idea to build a great library to his memory; that would have pleased him above everything else. Be sure his books are in it, and that the students are encouraged to read them, and not just to talk about them."

That same year a former employee of Will's, Ruth Garver Gagliardo, began the William Allen White Children's Book Award program. Her aim was to "honor the memory of the state's most distinguished citizen and to encourage Kansas children to read more and better books." Children themselves chose the winner from the finalists, making it the first first state children's book award of its kind in the nation. The White Award has since been copied by many other states.

Joining William Allen White and children's books came naturally for Mrs. Gagliardo. With her boss' encouragement, she wrote reviews of children's books for the *Gazette*, two years before any other newspaper in the nation did.

The White Award program follows an annual

Top: William Allen White Elementary in Emporia. The library at Emporia State University, above.

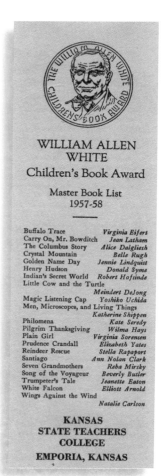

WILLIAM ALLEN WHITE

Children's Book Award

Master Book List
1957-58

Buffalo Trace	Virginia Eifert
Carry On, Mr. Bowditch	Jean Latham
The Columbus Story	Alice Dalgliesh
Crystal Mountain	Belle Rugh
Golden Name Day	Jennie Lindquist
Henry Hudson	Donald Syme
Indian's Secret World	Robert Hofsinde
Little Cow and the Turtle	
	Meindert DeJong
Magic Listening Cap	Yoshiko Uchida
Men, Microscopes, and Living Things	
	Katherine Shippen
Philomena	Kate Seredy
Pilgrim Thanksgiving	Wilma Hays
Plain Girl	Virginia Sorensen
Prudence Crandall	Elizabeth Yates
Reindeer Rescue	Stella Rapaport
Santiago	Ann Nolan Clark
Seven Grandmothers	Reba Mirsky
Song of the Voyageur	Beverly Butler
Trumpeter's Tale	Jeanette Eaton
White Falcon	Elliott Arnold
Wings Against the Wind	
	Natalie Carlson

**KANSAS
STATE TEACHERS
COLLEGE
EMPORIA, KANSAS**

cycle. Each fall a committee of children's literature professionals selects a list of books from those published for children the previous year. Each spring, children in grades three through eight vote for their favorite book from the list. A bronze award bearing the face of William Allen White, designed by Kansas sculptor Eldon Tefft, is presented to the winning author by a Kansas student in a ceremony each fall.

As it approached its 50th anniversary, the award was updated to reflect changes in children's literature and school structure. Two master lists of books are now selected. One is recommended for grades three to five and the other for grades six to eight. Children who have read at least two books on either or both lists may vote. Since 1952, more than 2,788,000 votes have been cast by the children of Kansas to select the annual winners of the White Book Awards.

When Kansas commissioned native sculptor Pete Felton to carve statues for the Kansas capitol of four Kansans who distinguished themselves, William Allen White was one of the chosen. His 2,000-pound statue was installed in 1981 on the second floor of the capitol in Topeka.

William Lindsay White, his wife Kathrine and their daughter Barbara moved into Red Rocks after Sallie's death in 1950 but spent much of their time in New York City and traveling abroad, continuing the "double life" of Will and Sallie. Kathrine proved to be a worthy partner to her husband in his career as Sallie had been to Will. A *Gazette* worker of the time said of W.L. White, "He never lost any interest in Emporia even though he didn't spend three months out of the year here for a good part of his life."

Top right: The medallion presented to the winner of the annual William Allen White children's book award. Above right: Statue in the rotunda of the Kansas Capitol.

Bill at a memorial to his father in El Dorado, Kansas. Kathrine at work at the Gazette.

Bill's redesign of the newspaper won a national award. When Barbara married David Walker in 1957, her reception took place at Red Rocks. When Bill's health began to fail, the Whites moved to Emporia permanently. In 1964 Bill attended the dedication of a memorial marker on the site of the large home Allen White built for his family in El Dorado. Shortly before Bill died at age 73 in 1973, Emporia honored him by renaming the Civic Auditorium the William Lindsay White Auditorium. When Bill died, Kathrine became the *Gazette*'s editor. Preferring to work behind the scenes, she brought an attention to detail to the job and assisted in restoring the *Gazette* building.

David Walker, left, and Barbara White Walker turned the William Allen White home over to the state of Kansas in 2001. Accepting was Gov. Bill Graves.

Barbara White Walker and David Walker took over the *Gazette* at the death of 85-year-old Kathrine in 1988. In 1995 they celebrated the 100th anniversary of her grandfather's purchase of it. Today, the fourth generation of the White family operates the *Gazette*; the editor and publisher is Christopher White Walker, a graduate of the William Allen White School of Journalism and Mass Communications at the University of Kansas. Next door to the *Gazette*, a small park dedicated to the memory of William Lindsay White includes a bust of him by sculptor Anne Spadea.

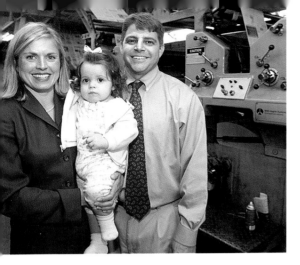

The current generation of Gazette leadership includes, from right, Christopher White Walker and Ashley Walker. They stood with one of their children, Grace, in the Gazette pressroom. Another daughter and a son have familar names: Hatten and William.

The White family's Colorado cabin became part of Rocky Mountain National Park when it was purchased in 1974 by the National Park Service. It now serves as an artist's retreat as part of an Artists in Residence program but still retains the name of William Allen White.

Travelers on the Kansas turnpike, I-35, learn about William Allen White if they stop at the Emporia rest area at milepost 132.

In 1937, Will made a prediction about the editorial he wrote after Mary's death, "Probably if her father has any sort of lasting fame beyond the decade following his death, it will come from this editorial." In 1977 that editorial formed the basis for an ABC-TV movie entitled "Mary White," which won an Emmy for outstanding writing and a Golden Globe nomination for best movie made for television. The movie, which was filmed in Emporia and surrounding towns and at Red Rocks, along with liberal quotations from the editorial brought Mary White and her family to life for a new generation.

Will's beloved Red Rocks also remains to bring him lasting fame. Placed on the National Register of Historic Places in 1971 and declared a National Historic Landmark in 1976, the home and its furnishings were donated to the Kansas State Historical Society in 2001 by Barbara White Walker and family and the Emporia *Gazette*. A federal grant and a lot of hard work brought the home and its gardens back to the beauty enjoyed by the Whites and their many guests. On May 14, 2005, more than 500 people attended the dedication of the William Allen White State Historic Site. Now tourists may enter the world created by the Whites' travels, love of books and delight in entertaining. Will's study still holds the desk at which he wrote, and in a nearby bedroom remains the bed in which presidents slept.

Left: The 1977 TV movie "Mary White." Above: Turnpike marker.

Dedication of the William Allen White State Historic Site.

"The house will let people know how he played a role in American history," his great-grandson Christopher White Walker commented.

Will once wrote, "Home is the most beautiful place in the world, for what is beauty but happiness?" How fitting that the home made beautiful by the Whites survives to bring happiness to people for years to come.

Recognition of William Allen White continues in the 21st century. He was named one of the four best editorial writers in American history by Michael Gartner in his book *Outrage, Passion, and Uncommon Sense: How Editorial Writers Have Taken on and Helped Shape the Great American Issues of the Past 150 Years* (Newseum 2005).

The Kansas Business Hall of Fame named him its 2006 Historical Honors Award recipient.

Bringing his own interpretations of national events, celebrating local achievements from glorious flower beds to new businesses, serving on local, state and national committees and leaving a lasting legacy through his writing, William Allen White towered in the world from his strong foundation in Emporia. Words he used to describe former Supreme Court justice Oliver Wendell Holmes in 1935 describe Will as well: "He escaped the warping with which fame twists many a man, and so he lived simply, naturally, beautifully to the end of a full and happy life."

And he did it all from Emporia.

Learn more about it

Websites:

The Emporia Gazette Family History: http://www.emporia.com/waw/index.html

William Allen White School of Journalism site: http://www.journalism.ku.edu/school/waw/index.html

William Allen White State Historic Site: http://www.kshs.org/places/white/index.htm

A Kansas Portrait: William Allen White: http://www.kshs.org/portraits/white_william.htm

The Rocky Mountain National Park Artist in Residence Program: http://www.nps.gov/romo/supportyourpark/artist_in_residence.htm

Videos:

Mary White. Paramount Home Entertainment. Released 1995. (Now on DVD)

The Story of William Allen White. Sagebrush Video Productions, PO Box 194, Nebraska City, NE 68410. Released 2000. http://www.sagebrushvideo.com

Source Notes

It was my intent to let William Allen White speak for himself as much as possible, so his *Autobiography of William Allen White* (New York: Macmillan, 1946) provided the greatest source for quotations. It will be abbreviated as WAW in these notes.

Likewise, quotations from his editorials in the Emporia *Gazette* were used. Its abbreviation will be EG.

White's autobiography ended with 1923, so I relied upon Walter Johnson's scholarly biography, *William Allen White's America* (New York: Henry Holt and Company, 1947) for information on later years. It will be abbreviated Johnson.

A large William Allen White collection on loan from the White family is housed in the Emporia State University Archives Special Collections, abbreviated ESU.

In her adulthood, Loverne Morris, a childhood neighbor of the Whites, recorded her memories, which supply wonderful detail for chapters six and seven. Morris, Loverne. "Little Girl Across the Street" (unpublished manuscript), Loverne Morris Papers, Emporia State University Archives will be abbreviated Morris.

Other White family material is on loan at Spencer Research Library at the University of Kansas, abbreviated KU.

Letters from the William Allen White Collection in the Library of Congress will be abbreviated LOC.

Introduction

7   "He hopes to always sign..." White, William Allen. "Entirely Personal". EG, June 3, 1895.

7   "To him the great world..." McCormick, Anne O'Hare. "Letter of Appreciation" from the dedication of the William Allen White Memorial Library booklet, 1952.

7   ..."an American institution". "William Allen White of Emporia: An American Institution is 70". *Life*, February 28, 1938, p. 9.

Chapter One

9   "There is another man..." WAW, p. 3.

10   "You can't say..." Letter from Allen White to Mary Ann Hatten, March 19, 1867. KU.

11   "The streets are full..." WAW, p. 20.

13   "...a pudgy, middle-sized boy..." *ibid*, p. 63.

14   Library records from letter from Conie Douglas, November 17, 1908. ESU.

14   "I have never ceased..." WAW, p. 85.

Chapter Two

15 "At fourteen..." WAW, p. 88.
16 "I used to go to their room..." *ibid*, p. 91.
16 "I was proud of him" *ibid*, p. 92.
17 "a big, healthy strapping..." *ibid*, p. 109.
19 "If I ever grew up..." *ibid*, p. 175.
22 "Sallie was always reading..." *ibid*, p. 255.
22 "My heart was in Kansas..." *ibid*, p. 256.

Chapter Three

26 "Suddenly I..." WAW, p. 284.
26 "It is a pleasure..." Bridges, Robert. *LIFE*, Jan. 7, 1897, pp. 6-7.
26 "I was always conscious..." WAW, p. 289.
27 "double life" *ibid*, p. 289.
27 "I had never known..." *ibid*, p. 297.
29 "We used to walk..." *ibid*, p. 324.
30 "...brown hair..." *ibid*, p. 326.

Chapter Four

32 "...I could not go out of Kansas..." Johnson, Walter, ed. *The Collected Letters of William Allen White*. New York, Henry Holt and Company, 1947, pp. 46-47.
32 "It has been assumed..." Canfield, Dorothy. "Country Editor...and Cosmopolite". Book-of-the-Month Club. In Memoriam. ESU.

Chapter Five

35 "...still yells loud" Letter from Sallie to William Lindsay White, August 26, 1904. KU.
36 "The editor of this paper..." "Wanted: A Horse" EG, April 3, 1906.
37 "When I walked..." WAW, p. 377.
39 " Even the humblest..." Clymer, Rolla A. "W.A. White—A Personal Estimate". Speech at February 22, 1952, dedication of KU school of journalism.
39 "I saw more of the pattern..." WAW, p. 407.
40 "...Mr. White is a journalist..." Johnson., p. 173. (See also Johnson's Collected Letters p. 100—letter dated March 21, 1909.)
40 Hotel bill reported by White, W.L. Address at dedication of William Allen White Library, 1952.
40 "Any Emporian's trip to Europe..." WAW, p. 406.

Chapter Six

43 "When your world..." Ferber, Edna. *A Peculiar Treasure*. New York: Doubleday, Doran & Company Inc., 1939, p. 227.
44 "When a neighbor..." Morris. Chapter Five, p. 4.
44 "A young *Gazette* employee" anecdote from Klintworth, Lawrence. *A Personal Glimpse of William Allen White*. El Dorado, Kansas: The Butler County Historical Society, 1983.
45 "Come to dinner..." Davids, Richard C. "At Home in the 'White' House of Emporia". *Better Homes and Gardens*. Vol. 20, No. 10. June 1942. pp. 15-17.
45 "It was a curious..." Audiotaped interview of W.L. White by Loren Pennington. Flint Hills Oral History Project. January 30, 1973. ESU.
46 "...was the spark plug..." Morris. Chapter Five, p. 4.
47 "...dive bomb the room..." Carle, Cecil. "Mary White's Brother Bill" (unpublished manuscript), Cecil Carle Papers, ESU, p. 12. Letter from Barbara White Walker to author May 12, 2006, described the lightning bugs.
47 "There were oceans of books..." Morris. Chapter Three, pp. 6-7.
47 "...incessant reading..." *ibid*, Chapter Four, p. 7.
47 "...they talked things over..." White, W.L. "The Sage of Emporia". William Allen White Centennial Speech, February 12, 1968, William Allen White School of Journalism, University of Kansas.
48 "When a house is adorned..." "Flowers and Things." EG, May 23, 1922.

49   "After breakfast at Red Rocks..." Morris. Chapter Three, p. 3.
49   "...to be in their home..." Gagliardo, Ruth Garver. "I Knew William Allen White". Address delivered at the 1967 meeting of the William Allen White Foundation. ESU.

Chapter Seven
52   Chicken dinner incident recounted in Morris. Chapter Twelve, pp. 83-84.
52   "The people of Emporia..." "Good Neighbors" EG, September 23, 1912.
53   "I saw a rotund..." Ferber, Edna. *A Peculiar Treasure.* New York: Doubleday, Doran & Company Inc., 1939.
53   "It was to be..." WAW, p. 461.
53   "No employee..." Lambert, Calvin. EG, February 1, 1944.
54   "Tell your story..." French, Laura. *Style Book for Reporters and Printers of the Emporia Gazette.* Adopted November 1, 1911, p. 4.
55   WAW's first attempt at driving is described in the Leonard and Gertrude Fort interview, "Reminiscences about William Allen White". June 29, 1966. ESU.
56   "I put him behind..." White, William Lindsay. "The Sage of Emporia". William Allen White Centennial Speech, delivered February 12, 1968, at the University of Kansas, p. 6.
56   "The house might..." Wright, Frank Lloyd to WAW, February 25, 1915. LOC.
56   "Wish list" described in Wright, Frank Lloyd to WAW, undated letter. LOC.
57   "Allen's home will be..." Wright, Frank Lloyd to WAW, August 25, 1916. LOC.
57   "Get reckless..." Wright, Frank Lloyd to WAW, September 28, 1916. LOC.
57   "...a great adventure..." WAW, p. 527.

Chapter Eight
59   "We should all remember..." "Save your Strafe". EG, April 13, 1917.
60   "...the story of two fat..." WAW, p. 535.
60   "...sitting down midway..." *ibid*, p. 626.
60   "Not since my father's death..." *ibid*, p. 551.
61   "In politics..." *ibid*, p. 578.
61   Story of red rock from audiotaped interview of W.L. White by Loren Pennington. Flint Hills Oral History Project Jan. 29, 1973. ESU.

Chapter Nine
65   Movie anecdote in Johnson , p. 344.
65   "Mary was full..." Morris, Loverne. "Life at Red Rocks, 1900-1918". *Kanhistique.* April 1979, p. 9.
66   "The whole student body..." Carle, Cecil. "Mary White's Brother Bill" (unpublished manuscript), Cecil Carle Papers, ESU, p. 13.
66   "Well, he'll never..." WAW, p. 604.
66   Account of Mary riding her horse into her grandmother's house is in Morris, Loverne. "Life at Red Rocks, 1900-1918". *Kanhistique.* April 1979, p. 9.
67   "She never had but one..." Leonard and Gertrude Fort interview, "Reminiscences about William Allen White". June 29, 1966. ESU.
67   "Mary has had another..." Johnson, p. 350.
68   "It was a long, sad..." WAW, p. 604.
68   "Tell me..." Carle, Cecil. "Mary White's Brother Bill" (unpublished manuscript), Cecil Carle Papers, ESU, p. 11.
68   "...we must..." Hinshaw, David. *A Man From Emporia.* New York: G.P. Putnam's Sons, 1945, p. 216.
69   "It has been..." WAW to Mrs. George Madden Martin . June 10, 1921. ESU.
69   "Probably if anything..." WAW, p. 605.
69   "...a brilliant affair..." WAW to W.L. White. May 10, 1922. LOC.

Chapter Ten
75   Use of Mary's upstairs room described in letter from Barbara White Walker to author, May 12, 2006.
76   "Mrs. White and I..." WAW to Mrs. George Madden Martin. June, 10, 1921. ESU.
76   "keeping up the game.." WAW to W.L. White, Oct. 14, 1921. LOC.
76   "Instead of 100 percent..." EG, June 19, 1922.

77   "The orderly business..." EG, July 27, 1922.
77   "The deepest friendship..." Johnson, p. 366.
77   "For nearly thirty years..." "Mary A. White". EG, May 7, 1924.

Chapter Eleven
80   "The K.K.K. people..." WAW to W.L. White, May 31, 1922. LOC.
80   "Always remember..." Clough, Frank. *William Allen White of Emporia*. New York: McGraw Hill Book Company, 1941, pg. 153.
81   "a stout little..." McCormick, Anne O'Hare. "Letter of Appreciation". Dedication of William Allen White Library booklet, 1952.
81   "You can't watch me..." Clough, Frank. *William Allen White of Emporia*. New York: McGraw Hill Book Company, 1941, p. 156.
82   "The kluxers..." "The Kluxers in Kansas" EG, May 5, 1926.

Chapter Twelve
86   "I have never had..." "Thoughts at 65". EG, February 11, 1933.
88   "Many persons living..." reported in Johnson, p. 485.

Chapter Thirteen
93   "...take off our ..." Johnson, pg. 538.
93   "The only reason..." Johnson, p. 544.
93   "...whatever you do..." WAW to J.S. Curry, March 31, 1941. ESU.
93   "...a place of pilgrimage." WAW to J.S. Curry, March 5, 1940. ESU.
94   "The job was..." Johnson, p. 547.
96   "Each day shows..." Sallie White to Victor Murdock, January 13, 1944. ESU
97   "Ask the boys..." Klintworth, Lawrence. "A Personal Glimpse of William Allen White". El Dorado, Kansas: The Butler County Historical Society, 1983, p. 1.
97   "The newspaper world..." Telegram from Franklin Delano Roosevelt to White family. January 29, 1944. ESU.
97   "...began to realize..." Klintworth, Lawrence. "A Personal Glimpse of William Allen White". El Dorado, Kansas: The Butler County Historical Society, 1983, p. 1.
98   William Allen White funeral described and Haskell's text in EG, Feb. 1, 1944.
98   "If he could have..." Klintworth, Lawrence. "A Personal Glimpse of William Allen White". El Dorado, Kansas: The Butler County Historical Society, 1983, p. 1.
98   "In the cemetery..." Johnson, p. 576.

Chapter Fourteen
100 "Behind nearly every..." "Mrs. Sallie White" EG, December 29, 1950.
101 "...to honor the memory..." Gagliardo, Ruth Garver. "I Knew William Allen White". Address delivered at the 1967 meeting of the WAW Foundation. ESU.
102 "He never lost..." Shupe, Ed, interview conducted by Loren Pennington. Flint Hills Oral History Project transcript, p. 18. March 19, 1974.
104 "Probably if her father..." White, William Allen. *Forty Years on Main Street*. New York: Farrar & Rinehart, Inc., 1947, p. 24.
105 "The house will let..." Manning, Carl. "The Sage of Emporia". (AP report) *The Wichita Eagle*. September 11, 2005, p. 2H.
105 "Home is the most..." "Beautiful Emporia". EG, April 26, 1901.
105 "He escaped the warping..." "Holmes Passes" EG, March 6, 1935.

Emporia State University Archives, Emporia State University:

William Allen White Collection, courtesy of Chris Walker: 1, 13 (upper left), 15 (lower left), 16 (right), 18 (left and lower right), 19, 20 (lower left), 21 (right), 24 (lower right), 27 (lower right), 29, 30, 34, 35, 36 (left), 37 (upper left), 40 (upper left), 41, 42, 45, 46 (upper left and right), 48, 50, 51, 52 (left), 53 (left), 55, 58, 61, 62, 64, 66-69, 70, 72, 73, 75, 77, 80, 82 (lower left), 83, 86, 88, 92 (right), 94, 96, 97 (lower right), 99, 100 (left and lower right), 103 (upper left and upper right).

Cecil Carle Collection: 47 (upper right)

Walter Anderson Collection: 24 (top), 104 (lower left).

Emporia *Gazette* and Barbara White Walker: 2, 7, 12 (upper left), 14 (lower left), 25, 27 (top right and lower left), 28 (upper left), 32 (bottom), 38, 49, 54 (bottom), 57, 76, 87, 90, 92 (left), 101 (middle right and lower right), 103 (upper right and lower right), 104 (upper left), 105.

Emporia *Gazette*, courtesy Diane and Rollin Post: 82.

University of Kansas Spencer Research Library, courtesy of Chris Walker: 6, 9, 10, 12 (bottom), 13 (upper and lower right), 14 (upper left and upper right), 15 (right), 17, 18 (upper right), 22, 46 (middle right and lower right), 60 (left), 63, 71.

Kansas City Star files: 8 (lower left), 21 (left), 23, 27 (middle right), 53, 78, 81, 84, 89, 93, 97 (upper right), 98 (right), 101 (left), 103 (lower right).

Kansas State Historical Society: Cover (map) and 8 (map), 16 (upper left), **52** (right)**,** 102 (lower right).

Tim Janicke, *Kansas City Star*: 31, 33, 37 (lower left and right), 47 (lower right).

Author: 40 (lower left), 60 (right), 74, 98 (left), 100 (upper right), 104 (right).

Butler County Historical Society: 12 (middle right), 103 (upper left).

Lyon County Historical Museum: 44.

All postcards from the collection of Loyette Polhans Olson.

Kansas City Public Library, Missouri Valley Special Collections: 20 (top).

INDEX

ACKNOWLEDGEMENTS

No nonfiction book is written in a vacuum. Although the scholarship and writing are mine, only the support and assistance of many others made this book a reality. To name them all is impossible, but they know who they are. Special thanks go to:

The family of William Allen White, whose granddaughter, Barbara White Walker, read my first draft and whose great-grandson, Chris Walker, granted permission to use archival material and complete access to the *Gazette's* many treasures, down to photos hanging on his office wall. This book would not have been possible without Mr. White's family being willing to share evidence of his achievements with a new generation.

Heather Wade began her work as archivist at Emporia State University the summer I began my research. Her professionalism, her expertise — and willingness to share it — made her an outstanding research companion.

Greg Jordan at the Lyon County Historical Museum, Brenda Lavington at the Lyon County Historical Archives, the staff at the Butler County Historical Society, Bobbie Athon, public information director for the Kansas State Historical Society, Kathy Lafferty and the staff at the University of Kansas Spencer Research Library, and the staff at the Rocky Mountain National Park storage facility all cheerfully played their part in helping me gather the images needed to illustrate Mr. White's story.

Roger Heineken of the William Allen White Community Partnership has been a cheerleader from early in my information-gathering. He's introduced me to some fine Emporia residents, and it's been fun swapping White stories and theories with him.

So many friends in the children's literature community encouraged me. Particularly, my friend Mary Jacob's insistence over the years that I should write a book gave me the confidence to try.

Being a children's librarian is the best job ever. My students past, present and future inspired the need for this book.

If I had chosen my own editor, I couldn't have done better than Star Books' Monroe Dodd. His appreciation of my text validated my writing ability, and his enthusiasm for the project matched my own. (His wife Jean's design work isn't too shabby, either.)

My friend, author Karen Epp, walked a parallel road with me and was great company.

My husband, Paul, selflessly supported me through the years this project required. More than anyone else, he listened to my theories, celebrated my finds, accompanied me on research trips, and never complained about "the other man" in my life.

It's been great fun sharing this project with my mother, Loyette Polhans Olson, whose own mother was from Emporia. Thanks, Mom, for creating in me a love of history and reading which culminated in this book.

All thanks to the Almighty whose hand I felt more than once guiding this project.